Shadows Of Acceptance

Nancy & Ron Rockey

Shadows Of Acceptance

Nancy & Ron Rockey

Published by eBookIt.com

ISBN-13: 978-1-4566-1064-7

Tribute

to

Ronald P. Rohner, Ph.D.
who has with great dedication and commitment
spent nearly half a century in research and study of
Parental Acceptance and Rejection
and to his wife
Nancy Rohner
who has faithfully worked beside him,
typing, teaching, collating information
and being supportive of her husband's work.

Without the steadfastness and devotion to this work,
many people would not come to understand
how a lack of acceptance causes devastation in a life.

We truly admire you and your work,
and are abundantly grateful for the
added insights your work has provided to
our calling - to provide tools for the
healing of rejection's effects.

May God Bless you both!

Table of Contents

Preface

"We live in the *Shadowlands*. The sun is always shining somewhere else. Round a bend in the road."

In one of our favorite films, *Shadowlands*, the true story of C.S. Lewis's life and marriage to Joy, Lewis speaks the above words. This famous sentiment seems to rightly depict the experience of most people – that joy, enlightenment and happiness is just around a bend, out of view, out of reach. The truth is that in order for there to be a shadow, the sun or light must be shining somewhere, so that a shadow can be cast. Could it be that light is right there in front or behind us, but because we predict that moving toward the light might be too painful, we choose to live only close to what could illuminate or make clear our understanding and progress? We live where we are, in one sense, comfortable, rather than pressing out into the unknown. Living in the shade, we are blinded by the light or we turn our back on it. It is predictable that in that artificial place, we will become gloomy, and perhaps see or comprehend only the outline or frosty image of the real, the true.

While people long for happiness, for the companionship of friends or family, for acceptance and the knowledge that they are cherished, still some illusion seems to keep from us, that which we long for most. An old experience or several of them, can become ghostly nightmares which haunt our present reality and paralyze us from action. Old slights experienced, old harsh words directed our way, old feelings that we were not wanted lurk in the darkness and we live in the shadow of the real, the longed-for dream. There in the scary world of the unknown or the partially seen, we languish, we suffer old hurts over and over again, until we lose sight of hope or a positive future.

The shadow of rejection is simply the flip side of the real – acceptance. It is the shadow, if you will, of the real object. Acceptance, the object for which we seek, seems to be held back by the shadow's fierce grip or blocked from view by a history of rejection. If we would step out of the shadow and into the light, we could see that the truth of acceptance has been present all the while. There has not been for one fraction of a second, even the slightest bit of rejection from the only source that really matters, yet even that truth has been hidden from view by one who loiters in the shadows reminding us of our unworthiness.

Stepping out into the light of truth however, dictates that we must really turn our backs to the lurking shadow, and that step requires just enough glimmering light to see that we are not stepping off a cliff into a deep chasm – just enough of truth to give us the courage to press forward. It requires just enough acceptance from somewhere to see that acceptance is indeed possible.

We are shaped by the way we think and feel, feeling coming before thinking. If our earliest feelings were of not belonging, not being wanted, not feeling loved and adored, our thoughts will follow when we are developed enough to think them. Those thoughts become our reality; they shape our attitudes toward our own value and our behaviors toward others. Knowledge alone will begin to enlighten the shadowlands, that place where, as Lewis says, our happiness is just beyond a bend in the road where the sun must be shining. Let's dare to walk together out of our shadows and into the light.

Introduction

Devastating, wasn't it, being the only one who didn't get an invitation to the birthday party or the big wedding? Maybe your heartache was being the ignored child in your family, and your sibling got all the attention, the new clothes or toys. Did you always end up with the hand-me-downs? Perhaps you had "two left feet," so to speak, so all of the other girls but you were asked to dance. Or were you a clumsy one who ended up being the last to be picked for the baseball team? What anguish! Perhaps you were just an inconvenience and your parent(s) kept telling you to "get lost." Oh maybe not in those words, but in other ways. One fellow we know had an absent father and a mother who would shoo him out of the house with these words: "Don't come home until the streetlights come on." Wasn't that the same message as if she had said – "I don't want you here?"

There it is – that bone-chilling word – rejection. The sound of it conjures up memories of slights received and of tears shed. With it comes the poor self-worth that arrives as a result. "There must be something wrong with me. What have I done or said to be cast off like yesterday's underwear?" Here is the shadow, the dimness that hides from view the possibilities of living a life of true acceptance.

There's more than just an emotional response to feeling unwanted; there is also the physical response of a gut-ache or heartache. Ever been there? Some who feel unloved will comfort themselves by eating everything in sight, while others can't eat a thing! Some will rush to a comfy spot for a long winter's nap, while others can't sleep a wink; their minds racing with negative and painful thoughts. Others may lash out at those close to them, yelling and cursing at them about the abuse they've received. Some will crawl out of harm's way into a cave of their own making, keeping destructive thoughts and feelings inside them, while retreating to an assumed place of safety. Others may be driven to work endlessly, hoping that their accomplishments will make them feel accepted. Years may pass after the initial discounting or dismissal by a parent or some other significant person in a child's life, but the pain of that negative treatment looms in the shadow of a life thus unfulfilled. Whenever a slight occurs later in life, be it a huge rejection or one barely noticed, those same painful feelings arise. With each succeeding rebuff, the hurt escalates in intensity and so does the reaction to it!

Most of the responses to rejection are self-destructive. The torture of keeping a mental list of abuses received only piles up resentment and bitterness with the list. Paralysis increases. Eventually, an explosion of catastrophic dimensions will occur with fallout landing on either oneself or on those with whom a victim is in closest relationship. Retaining slights or purposeful rejections, which one cannot help but do, especially because they are emotionally charged, constructs a set of grey, cloudy glasses worn every day by the victim and used to predict and prevent reactions from all they meet.

Why should this be? It is because the brain has a method of working, a design to help us to be protected and have the ammunition to combat further rejections. The only issue here, is that those attacks keep piling up and eventually can cause volcanic-type eruptions when we least expect them.

Furthermore, those reactions and eruptions bring to us the very rejection that we fear.

Alice Miller, a widely-published and well-known author, has achieved world-wide recognition for her work on the causes and effects of child abuse and its cost to society. In her book entitled *The Drama of Being a Child,* first published in 1987 and revised in 1995, she states:

> "Experience has taught us that we have only one enduring weapon in our struggle against mental illness: the emotional discovery of the truth about the unique history of our childhood."

She continues:

> "The truth is so essential that its loss exacts a heavy toll, in the form of grave illness. In order to become whole we must try, in a long process, to discover our own personal truth, a truth that may cause pain before giving us a new sphere of freedom. If we choose instead to content ourselves with intellectual 'wisdom', we will remain in the sphere of illusion and self-deception."

Powerful words, aren't they? But oh so true! The history contained in the Old Testament is a referral tool, designed for us to use so that we will not repeat the errors of our forefathers. There is always a precipitating event producing inhibitions and fear, but it is possible to break through the shadow of the past and into the light of accomplishment, success and emotional growth. Your interest in the subject of rejection is, therefore, a path of wisdom. Your physical and emotional health will greatly benefit from your choice to face your feelings, head on.

The ways that we connect or plug in to each other are greatly influenced by the shadows created from our early experiences of attaching to primary caregivers in childhood, and that attachment is determined by how those parents or primary caregivers were equipped to bond with us. Because our need to survive is so strong, it has determined how or if we will attach to others in our lives in a secure manner. Our ability to attach or to plug in has also been impacted by the wounds we received while we were in the process of determining our worth and value. The first two years of life are the most impactful, but up to age 7 is when our thoughts and feelings are formed.

Let's face it, the bottom line is this: wounded people wound people. Rejected people look for rejection under every rock, and nearly always find it. If they do not find it, they create it, by behaving in such a manner that others will reject them. Their shadow enlarges.

The forty-five years of study in parental rejection and acceptance, conducted by Dr. Ronald Rohner of the University of Connecticut's Family Studies Department, concludes that if a person *perceives* he is rejected, he has received it. One's perception is one's reality.

So, if in your character-forming years (conception through age 7) you felt like you did not belong to your family and friends, or if you currently find yourself being sensitive to the slights of others, predicting that friends or family will reject you, you are in the right place! There is so much more to learn and apply to yourself on this subject.

So now, let's move on!

Chapter One

Unplugged

"The greatest terror a child can have is that he is not loved, and rejection is the hell he fears. I think that everyone in the world to a large or small extent has felt rejection. And with rejection comes anger, and with anger some kind of crime in revenge for the rejection, and with the crime – guilt - and there is the story of mankind."

(The Rejected. 10). Evoy, John Joseph

Picture it. You were given away at birth by a father who wouldn't even claim you as his, or by a mother who was so young that she had no idea about the needs of an infant and had no ability to meet those needs if she did know them. Perhaps she didn't really want the responsibility of raising a child. She may have wished to have an abortion but didn't have the money to have it done. She may have even tried to abort you herself by means that had been suggested to her by others, but her attempts were unsuccessful. Maybe she was unmarried and/or so young that she knew she should tell her parents but was scared to death to confess the truth, for fear of the putdowns and demands she would get from them. She could have been so totally caught up in the trauma of an unplanned and unwanted pregnancy that she had no thought of connecting with the child in her womb and probably wouldn't have known how to anyway. Most women don't, regardless of age or status.

The human brain is designed to see to it that the mind and the body will survive at all costs. As a result, through the years the brain will develop techniques to keep the human alive and functioning. In the first two years of life, when the mind is like a giant sponge that soaks in information, your style of attachment was developed. The choice you made was dependent on your mother and father's abilities to bond to you in the womb. It became a survival technique, designed to protect you from the results of wounding. Each of the self-protective techniques you may have developed carries a price. In addition to difficult future relationships, came the current cost of dealing with personal attitudes and feelings that may not serve you well now.

When a child is abandoned by birth parents, even while still in the womb, that child, unable to articulate the pain it feels, develops several reactions to its experience of being alone. Abandonment can mean actually giving the child up for adoption, to foster care, or even just leaving the infant on someone's doorstep or in a dumpster, emotionally abandoning or ignoring the child while still being physically present, leaving the child orphaned due to death or divorce, having extended periods of absence of one or both parents due to work-related concerns, removing love and acceptance from the child because of its birth being inconvenient to the parents, being disappointed by the sex of the child, or being pre-occupied with marital strife, addictions or other pursuits. Our shadows, our resulting feelings and behaviors, owe their birth to the light of our beginnings.

Main Reactions to Rejection

Feelings of Worthlessness:

When a child endures a difficult delivery, or his needs are unmet, he or she is abused, physically, emotionally or sexually or he or she has to endure painful experiences of loss or abandonment, the child draws a conclusion and develops an attitude about his worth and value. “If my mother or my father, who created me, would treat me in a hurtful way, then there must be something wrong with me.” Granted, this is not true; however, what the child perceives he receives as truth. Looking at it from a logical adult point of view, his reaction would not be unexpected. If you were beaten severely, if you were ignored or left alone to amuse yourself while your parents pursued other things, if you were sexually abused by a parent or another, if you were repeatedly told that you were dumb or stupid or were called degrading names, if you were seldom or never touched, caressed, rocked or cuddled, you would consider yourself to be less than what your parents wanted or hoped for. You would feel that you were the problem.

“But wait a minute,” you might say. “I haven't been severely beaten, given away shortly after birth, and my mother didn't attempt to abort me. There was nothing **that** dramatic going on in my household, but I still feel that I was rejected, so what's wrong with me?” The answer: probably there was a more subtle form of rejection going on for you, one that is not easily identified, but felt none-the-less. Again, the truth is that if you perceived that you were rejected, then you received rejection as your truth.

Todd attended one of our seminars and expressed this exact sentiment. "Outwardly my parents seemed to accept me, at least they didn't hurt me in any way, physically or emotionally. There were no mean words hurled my direction, but still I feel rejected," he said. Upon questioning him further, we discovered that both of his parents were busy professionals and pre-occupied with their professions. Todd was left to amuse himself most of the time. He did get healthy meals, usually on time (there was a strict routine at his home), but attention was more on their professional life than on family life. Also, if there was attention given out, it was to the eldest sister, who they were grooming, so it seemed to Todd, to be someone very special.

Children don't usually assume the worst of their parents. In actuality the reverse is true, because every child longs to belong, to be accepted. It might have been that one or both of your parents were very busy with their careers and you didn't receive the attention or the amount of time with them that you needed. Children always feel that they are to blame for inadequate attention, and will feel rejection as a result. You do not have to be claiming a dramatic story of abuse or neglect to have experienced rejection. Read on, and you may find yourself identified in what's ahead.

A child longs for an intimate emotional bond with his parents: affectionate and tender treatment from a warm and loving Mom and Dad. When this does not occur, the child takes the blame for the neglect. God designed newborns to be helpless, in need of everything being done for them. If a child is raised with affectionate parents who give the child love and attention, the child is able to remove himself from the "center of attention" position to become part of a supportive system to everyone he knows and primarily to God. For those who have been wounded by rejection, neglect and/or abuse however, this center-stage position often remains until puberty and/or into adulthood, always seeking to be the center of attention, always looking to have his needs met. Remember, the brain is designed for survival, so the adult child (one who never matured emotionally because of his negative experiences) says, "I have to have these needs met somehow, so I will demand that of everyone."

The shadow of rejection causes victims to perceive many of the words said to them as slights, neglect or outright rebuff, and they respond out of their perception instead of reality. His or her attitude will be that the world "owes" him, and that can be the case into adolescence, adulthood and even into senior years. The child will mature physically but not emotionally. This is known as "Arrested Emotional Development," and lives in the shadow as a result of rejection and other abuses as well.

Feelings of worthlessness manifested in a school-age child are shown in extremes. Emotions are intense. The extroverted child will be obnoxiously out front and "in your face", while the introverted child will "disappear into the woodwork," so to speak. He/she will have either little or no desire to excel in school work, or will be a perfectionist, always performing for acceptance. The pendulum swing can be extreme. In either extreme, parents get concerned and attempt to "fix" the problem – the child. This concern, when the child is being made into the problem or the patient, further diminishes self-worth and can drive a child into a deeper hole of emotional pain.

In adolescence, emotions intensify creating either the rebellious, mouthy teen or the "geek"-- the shy, quiet, intellectual who has few or no friends. This is the time period when a teen's work is to begin to separate and be different from parents. It is the phase called **identity development**, and is extremely difficult for parents. In childhood there may have been an adequate relationship with parents, but in adolescence, the teen wants to be with peers and seldom with his parents. This is a normal part of adolescent development. The wounded teen will experiment with and may get hooked on agents that will allow him to escape from the negativity that he feels, or he will lash out in behaviors that are destructive to self and to others. Teens may also escape into video games or computers to avoid associations that "might" cause pain. Schoolwork is an area where teens feel they have power – either to perform to the max being straight "A" students or to slack off, getting poor grades just to get back at parents or to be in control of oneself. It has also been noted in numerous studies that wounds tend to "dumb down" intellect or diminish academic performance, especially in the elementary and secondary school years.

Worthlessness in adult years has many behaviors, because by now, the wounded have experienced enough of life to be committed to the idea of their own worthlessness. Experiences endured thus far have "proved the point" to this teen, even though his actions may demonstrate that he considers himself superior to others. Behaviors run the gamut from absolute perfectionism and control, including obsessive and compulsive behaviors to an "I don't care" attitude where little or nothing is accomplished or achieved. Goals are set either very high (unreachable) or very low (absent). Relationships are based either on performing for the marital partner or boss for acceptance or not being responsible and not caring for oneself or one's partner. Careers are impacted so that either the victim becomes a super-achiever or never really accomplishes much in life and contributes little or nothing of value to society.

Depression and hopelessness are the resulting feelings when self-worth is based on one's abilities to perform in a certain manner.

Perhaps by now you have begun to comprehend the importance of one's self-concept. It is the pivot point on which a child becomes a success or a failure in life.

Self-concept is a personal view of one's worth and value. It's what you think that you are worth.

Self-image is based on the reflection that one sees of himself based on the attitudes and behaviors of others toward him. An image is a reflection – a picture coming back at you in the mirror of others.

Self-worth is the innate (inborn) value you have just because you exist. That value is placed on you by your Creator, and never changes despite your behaviors or beliefs. Each life has value, regardless of who the parents are or from what lineage you have come. Life is precious!

Self esteem is a holding of oneself in high regard – perhaps to think more highly of oneself than one ought to think. It is to have a high regard for self, perhaps to think that self is superior to another.

Having had a look at these definitions, ask yourself what your self-concept is. Unfortunately, we usually base our concept on the earliest relationships we have had in life -– those with our parents or primary care-givers. Our concept of our worth and value gets tied up with the image returned to us from those who related to us in infancy. Their behaviors toward us set us up to believe a lie, and unwittingly we believe that image over what our Creator would have us see.

Believing the lie that we are without worth and value or that it is minimal at best, is the set up for a plethora (excess) of relational, career and personal failures. Holding onto a lie as truth is the stimulus for us to create an entire language based on the lie. We will either proclaim our depraved state or we will cover up our feelings with an air or appearance of superiority. Attitudes translate into behaviors designed to portray or to conceal the lie, and unfortunately many of these behaviors are destructive to self and can be damaging to others.

If you have been trapped in the lie that says you have little or no worth and value, it's time to get out of the shadows and into the light of freedom you will feel when you comprehend the incredible innate value that you have.

Fear:

Everyone is born with a few basic fears such as falling and loud noises. All of our fears, whether they are real or just perceived, come from the conclusions we have formed about ourselves, the world around us, and the people in it.

Real fear is healthy, protective fear and is based on a valid conclusion about the world and its people. It can prevent us from choosing behaviors that will bring us harm, anxiety or other discomfort. It can, for example, prevent us from stepping into a poorly shaped and slippery bathtub without a rubberized mat to prevent a fall or walking out into a busy street without looking both ways first.

Mythical fear comes from faulty and self-defeating conclusions we form when we are trying to cope with toxic input from our culture or family. It is also a prediction of what will happen if we don't make a particular choice. It is both limiting and destructive, and can prevent us from enjoying every day pleasures and relationships. Obsessions and compulsions often stem from this type of fear.

The brain is most impressionable in the first two years of life and learns seventy-five percent of all that is needed for life during that time. Our earliest messages are received through our emotions and experiences, and the most powerful and long-lasting of these become the foundation for our later thoughts, feelings and behaviors.

A difficult birth can make a lasting impression on the Reticular Activating System, which creates the set-point for the muscle tension or hyper-alertness in the body at the time of birth. If birth was complicated and the child's life was in danger, fear kick-starts the Reticular Activating System, located at the base of the brain, and the infant's muscles are set on tight or tense, and fear creates emotional tenseness, making the child anxious. The experiences of childhood or later life can increase or decrease the set point of the body's tension. It should be noted that it is easier to increase the tension than it is to decrease it.

Origins of fear include:

1. Innate - Inborn (falling, loud noises etc.)
2. Frightening experiences in the womb (mother or child's health)
3. Mother's fears transferred through hormones to fetus
4. Reality – frightening experiences of life.
5. Faulty conclusions drawn about the world and its relation to us
6. Childhood modeling of primary caregiver's fears.
7. Thoughts created and exaggerated from past memories
8. Perceptions – usually subtle associations from experiences
9. Body sensations which stimulate and cellular memories -- the language of the body telling us that arousal is occurring
10. Fictitious tales told to us by others, i.e. the "Boogy Man"

There are really only two basic emotions: love and fear. Fear drives all negative, self-protective and harmful emotions. Some people are totally controlled by their fears, and therefore miss out on a great deal of happy living. Fears make us control freaks, macho men, hysterical women and selfishness, jealousy, envy, anger, and a host of other unpleasant attitudes are ours to experience as a result of fear.

According to Alice Miller in her book, *The Drama of Being a Child,*

> ". . . a child who was heavily traumatized at the beginning of his life will be in particular need of care and attention in order to overcome the fears arising out of more recent experiences" (34).

So, ask yourself when a fear arises: "Is this real or mythical?" "Where in childhood did this fear come from?" "If love is the opposite of fear, what would love do in this situation? Is it possible for me to break out of the shadow and into the light of courage and love?

Anger:

Does anger come easily for you? Can you feel it rising within you at the slightest provocation? Do you hand it out to others or do you bury it deep inside you, allowing it to seethe and build as you continually rehearse in your mind the injustice you feel you have received?

Anger can be both healthy and destructive to the human mind and body. *Healthy anger* feels an injustice either received personally or dished out to another, and responds by taking some positive action to remedy the injustice. *Destructive anger* either reacts, lashes out with negative action or it is repressed, and seethes within causing internal stressors that are harmful to both the mind and the body. Built up resentments and bitterness create nasty dispositions!

Remember that the brain is designed to see to it that the mind and the body will survive? Anger is a survival technique. When anger rises in the human, the adrenal glands produce adrenalin to give the body needed energy to fight or to flee. The adrenals also produce nor-adrenalin and cortisol, two additional stress hormones needed for the body's reaction to a threat. However, when the adrenal glands produce these hormones in large amounts and when there is no need to actually run or physically fight, they are destructive to the body.

Danny's anger had raged inside of him from years of physical and emotional abuse received from his father and from repeatedly seeing his mother physically abused by the same perpetrator. When his mother's death was eminent due to breast cancer that had metastasized to numerous parts of her body, Danny blamed his father for her illness. His rage prompted him to threaten his father's life, planning his murder in detail. Not heeding the counsel to get psychological help to eradicate his rage, he contained it until it exploded internally and destroyed his physical body. What a loss! A thirty-two year old man, drug and alcohol free, a powerful athlete, executed by his own anger that hid in the shadows of his daily experiences, and showed itself whenever he felt rejection again.

On the other hand, *Anger can be valuable.* It can cause the needed adrenalin rush to combat a threat, but when it is contained, the overload of adrenal hormones can destroy a life.

Anger and the Brain

It is very helpful to know that the computer-like brain stores experiences and the emotions produced by those experiences. When an event occurs in the present that has within it elements reminiscent of past anger producing experiences, our reactions are not just from the present situation, but from all similar, anger-producing past events. Let's offer an example: Let's say that you have had years of being called derogatory names by your father. Now you are working in a corporation where your boss has a short fuse and frequently demeans you, calling you names. You have responded by retreating and absorbing blame. However, one day, he is on a toot and doing his usual raging, and seemingly from nowhere your rage breaks out. You yell, scream obscenities and finally stomp out, quitting your job. You were reacting to all past injustices received from him plus those from your earlier experiences. It was not just the emotions of the day that you were feeling, and that's why your rage was "over the top!" You were carrying old baggage with you, and it exploded along with your current anger. You see, the mind works that way. It's designed to remember, not to forget, and when a stimulus comes from either inside you or from an outside source, you automatically go into your memory bank and very rapidly file through your memories, tagging each one that in any way reminds you of the present stimulus. Then you react from the current injustice and every other injustice you have experienced. That's why it's so easy to "blow a gasket!"

Rejection and Anger

One of the most common and explosive anger-producing experiences is the feeling of being rejected. If you experienced rejection early in childhood, especially from an intimate relationship such as parent-child, it becomes a filter through which every other relationship is seen, and it lurks in the shadow of your history. *Rejected people look for rejection under every rock and usually find it.* If they do not find it, they tend to manufacture it – conjure it up in their minds. Much anger stems from the feeling of being unjustly treated. Rejection is unjust, so when it is experienced it produces anger. The anger can be displayed outwardly or buried deep within the mind. What happens, however, is that the anger usually seeps out in nasty digs or comments directed toward the one who did the rejecting, even if it is buried deeply. One way or another, anger gets expressed, even if it's expressed in the development of illnesses and in the attitude of an individual.

Anger can be a beneficial emotion as long as it is expressed in an appropriate manner. It can create healing, harmony, and/or reconciliation if it is not expressed with the intent to cause injury or harm.

Sadness or Depression:

If you were the victim of childhood abuse, if you were ignored or unwanted, put down, beaten or sexually violated, it would be normal if you would consider yourself to be the cause of all that happened to you. According to you, you are the problem or you could have/should have prevented the problem.

Children, being at the center of their universe, either take the blame or the credit for all that comes to them. If you blamed yourself for the abuse you received, this would easily create sadness or depression within you. Depression is basically anger turned inward toward oneself. "If I weren't so bad, these terrible things would not befall me." A sense of hopelessness ensues. A black cloud hovers or a shadow follows wherever you are.

A mother who cannot recognize the needs of her child or fulfill them, is no doubt in need herself. She, therefore, endeavors to fill her own needs through the child. What the child needs to receive, the mother cannot give, and so he doesn't develop the framework in which he can develop, identify and feel his own feelings and emotions. This can easily be the cause of a child not "being himself" for the rest of his life. It becomes easy for this person to live in the past and to respond to today's experiences as if they were in the past. Decisions are made based on what his mother would want him to choose. This person can easily lose his sense of self.

A "poor me" attitude -- feeling despair because the world will not devote itself to making you happy -- keeps the individual-you- the victim. The one who has in the past or currently is causing wounds is in control of the individual and his/her emotions. Living "under the circumstances" or in the shadows, rather than being in control of one's life and decisions, assigns the power to the perpetrator.

Granted, a victim of abuse has a right to be sad regarding the treatment received, however each person also has the responsibility to rise above the circumstances, to take control of his life and his future, and to insure that those close to them live in peace. No one else can do it. This is where a decision and a determination to escape from the haunting shadow is necessary, and one has to know what is in the shadow and how it controls the present. Then, and often with help from a professional, a decision to escape can be made.

Depression is a state like being on a merry-go-round that revolves faster and faster, making one dizzy and totally out of control. The more pondering of the past and the abuses experienced, the deeper the depression and the sense of hopelessness gets. This is why so many people need recovery from the past hurts they've endured as well as a determination to move ahead. It is an intervention designed to turn off the tape recording in the brain and to slow or stop the merry-go-round so that your sense of stability and equilibrium can be found. Recovery is the light directed toward the shadow illuminating the darkness.

Depression hijacks the ability to think in a logical or positive manner, and, sometimes, chemical intervention is necessary to redeem chemical balance in the brain and body in order to return the ability to think logically and positively. Often, a well qualified and experienced therapist can assist by helping someone with clinical depression to regain the ability to think in a realistic and positive manner. In such cases, chemical intervention may be needed for a time until old issues can be safely resolved. In a recovery process, identifying the real causative element of depression and removing the negative emotional charge lurking in the shadow from old memories of pain, brings relief.

Attachment Influenced by Abuses Received:

All of the wounds received in childhood, especially in the first two years, carry with them the after-effects of worthlessness, fears, anger and sadness and form the shadow that follows you. The shadow exaggerates your reactions to other abuses received. If you have been abused early on in life, you may avoid close interactions with others or will cling desperately to one who feels safe to you. You may also be disorganized in your attachment, avoiding at times and clinging at other times.

In the first two years of life, we unknowingly choose our style of attachment, and that choice is powerfully influenced by what we have experienced during the early months of life. The steady or frequent absence of a parent, compounded by abuse, leads a child far away from being able to securely attach and toward one of the three dysfunctional styles of attachment. This choice is a survival technique as well.

Why do Parents reject their children?

<u>Mothers:</u>

1. Maladjusted marriages–the poorer the marriage, the less acceptance of the child
2. Arrival of another child who is the preferred gender or is more physically attractive to mother
3. Infant closely resembled a self-loathing parent
4. Children resembled "the other side of the family" whom the parent resents.
5. Untimely pregnancies -- infant considered an unwanted or unjust imposition
6. Child became a "stand-in for the other parent, rather than receiving affection in his own right
7. Latent hostility was unconsciously displaced from parent's own rejecting parents to the child
8. Parents employed a hands-off policy with their children – to the point of neglect - due to being over-dominated by their own parents
9. Immediate identification of the child with the child's father – especially true for unwed mothers

10. Mother couldn't afford the emotional risk involved in loving a child, especially in cases where another child had been lost in death
11. Child was viewed as anchoring a couple to a difficult marriage
12. Viewed the child as an intruder with whom she was forced to share her husband. This is especially true if the mother had experienced rejection
13. Felt that the child had deprived her of a job or career that she enjoyed – having a child felt like a loss of freedom
14. Mother had major emotional or mental issues, that have been inadequately addressed.

Fathers:

1. Maladjusted marriage
2. Child was physically or psychologically unattractive
3. An untimely pregnancy
4. Close resemblance to their loathed selves
5. Close resemblance to their mate's despised relatives
6. Jealousy
7. An inability to love
8. An unconscious repayment back to his own parents
9. Feeling of personal inadequacy

10. Promiscuity that cannot be satisfied with only one partner- feels tied down.
11. Questioning whether they had married the right woman.
12. Man had mental or emotional issues that have been inadequately treated.

*These lists were taken from Dr. Joseph Evoy's book, *The Rejected.* (25-31)

Of all the recorded abuses, rejection seems to carry the most pervasive and detrimental effects. Keep in mind however, that even after recovery, the memories of rejecting experiences remain, but the negative emotional charge, which drives feelings and behaviors, will be removed from those memories. When a slight occurs in the present, it can bring up a rejection you experienced in the past, but your response to it will be mitigated because of your recovery. It'll be entirely different! You will just notice it and move on! Without recovery, only the *Shadows of Acceptance* are our norm.

Chapter Two

The Brain and the Mind

Before proceeding further, we would like you to learn a bit about the human brain and the mind. The brain has been referred to as a "3 pound universe." Actually that is quite aptly stated because it controls all the function of the body. Without it, a person cannot exist. A person's life would be totally without experience and enthusiasm, if it weren't for the healthy functioning of the mind and the health of the brain.

This section may seem a bit technical; however, if you use the diagram found on page 10 it may help you to decipher where the different parts of the brain are located. This will be great reference material in the future and is placed here for your further learning.

Structure and Function:

The brain and the spinal cord make up what is known as the central nervous system. Both are housed within bony structures. The brain is located inside the skull and the spinal cord is housed in the multiple vertebrae of the spinal column. There are numerous regions of the brain that have specialized functions

The Spinal Cord:

The spinal cord is a long, tapering structure that lies within the curved enclosure of the spinal vertebrae. It receives information transmitted from the many nerves of the skin, joints, muscles and ligaments, and it sends out messages for motor movements. If the spinal cord is cut or severed due to injury, sensations and voluntary movements are lost in the parts of the body governed by nerve impulses below the injury.

The Brain Stem:

The brain stem has three components –

1. *The Medulla* – Only an inch long of tissue, the medulla is located at the place where the spinal cord enters the brain stem. It controls such tasks as: breathing, talking, singing, swallowing, vomiting and the maintenance of blood pressure and, in part, the heart rate.
2. *The Pons (Bridge)* – Located just above the medulla, the pons is a broad band of fibers that link the cerebellum and the cerebral cortex.
3. *The Midbrain* – This is the smallest part of the brain stem and it is continuous from the pons. It permits elemental forms of seeing and hearing. The *cerebellum* lies directly behind the pons, and is chiefly concerned with modulating the range and force of movements. Without it, you would not be able to move an object without dropping it.

The Diencephalon:

Includes the thalamus and the hypothalamus –

1. *Thalamus* – The thalamus processes all of the senses except smell.

2. *Hypothalamus* – Located directly beneath the thalamus, it is the regulatory center for many vital activities, some of which are outside of conscious awareness such as vital endocrine amounts, water balance, sexual rhythms, food intake and the autonomic nervous system. It is also the command center for many complex mood and motivational states, such as anger, fatigue, placidity (state of calmness) and hunger.

The Limbic System:

Also called the emotional, primitive or old brain

The Limbic System is a network of nerve centers above the hypothalamus with connections to both the cortical centers in the temporal lobe that are concerned with higher thought and higher cognitive (thinking) functions and the hypothalamus. It is involved with the same emotional states. The dual relationship allows emotions to reach conscious awareness where cognitive fantasies and observations can affect us emotionally. In other words, the emotions affect the thinking and the thinking affects the emotions.

The Cerebral Hemispheres:

There are two hemispheres of the brain, and they are involved with our highest motor and conceptual functions. They consist of the overlaying **cerebral cortex,** the **basal ganglia**, which works with the cerebellum to coordinate body movements, and three large nuclear groups – the **caudate nucleus**, the **putamen** and the **pallidium. The cerebral cortex** is actually **the** gray, wrinkled cerebrum, which is about as thick as corrugated cardboard, and contains approximately 10-14 billion neurons. Beneath the cerebral cortex are the four central lobes of the brain.

The two hemispheres resemble each other – like two halves of a walnut. Each hemisphere is divided into separate territories: the **frontal**, the **parietal**, the **occipital** and the **temporal** lobes. However, contrary to what was previously thought, the boundaries between lobes and hemispheres are not particularly distinct.

Frontal Lobe – is concerned with movement and the formation of complex motor "programs." The most forward portion of this lobe, the **prefrontal fibers**, is concerned with personality, insight and foresight. It exerts an inhibitory control over our actions, bringing them into line with social expectations. Injuries to this area may cause socially unacceptable behaviors. An injury, to the motor cortex, such as a stroke, can cause paralysis.

Parietal Lobe – contains the primary sensory cortex – the feeling part of the brain which receives impulses from all the body's sensory receptors. It is concerned with processing tactile (touch) information, language comprehension and complex aspects of time orientation.

Temporal Lobe - is important for hearing, memory, and a person's sense of self and time. 'De ja vu' experiences originate here, and, because it is connected to the limbic system, the temporal lobe plays an important part in emotional experiences. Visceral or intuitive responses are found here as are learning and memory recall.

Occipital Lobe – is the visual center of the brain. It carries out extraordinarily complex transformations of the information transferred from the retina of the eye. Here a person takes in the sight of an object, and the transforming process identifies what the object is and how to relate to it. A stroke or injury here can cause severe visual impairment or blindness.

The two hemispheres look very much alike, but they process information in different ways.

The **right hemisphere** operates holistically, so forming a mental picture of ones living room is done best by the right side. It is best in visual-spatial tasks such as forming mental maps, recognizing the face of a friend, or rotating geometrical objects.

The **left hemisphere** excels in breaking things down into their component parts such as mentally counting the number of chairs in a room, and then the types or colors of chairs.

Remember, that both hemispheres work best together in cooperation with each other for maximum functioning.

Do you recall that the human brain is designed to remember and not to forget? Remembering what was in the past is a part of the survival mechanism on which the brain insists. We recall the way we did things in the past, so that we can repeat what worked and delete what did not work. We recall past experiences that were pleasurable in order to replicate the experience, thus creating more pleasure. We remember what was painful or hurtful so that we can avoid it in the present or the future.

Actually, the brain works on a formula similar to the one identified by Dr. Pavlov, who used a German Shepherd, a dinner bell and a piece of raw meat. The scientist showed the meat to his dog and simultaneously rang a dinner bell. The response of the dog was that he salivated. After repeating this experiment several times, Pavlov approached the dog and rang the bell but did not present the dog with the meat. The dog still salivated. From that experiment Pavlov created the famous formula: "Stimulus yields response."

The brain works similarly. A stimulus is presented to us – it can be a memory from the past or a sight, sound, taste, touch or smell in the present. Automatically, the brain enters its "filing cabinet" of all past memories and files through them at an amazingly rapid rate. The old memories that in any way relate to the current stimulus are "tagged" and we respond to the one memory that is most highly charged with emotion. Say, for example, you were attacked in childhood by a swarm of bees and were bitten by several, necessitating a trip to the emergency room and a shot of a powerful antihistamine to lessen your body's reaction. Today you are having lunch with a friend at a lovely outdoor restaurant surrounded with flowers, and you see a bee lighting on the rose nearest to you. You jump up from the table, clutch your chest with one hand and wildly wave your napkin with the other. Your friend wonders what in the world struck you, and so do the folk at tables around you. Others have seen the bee, but they ignore it and go on eating their lunch.

All it took for you was the sight of one bee, and your mind went into its filing cabinet, pulled out "bee", chose the emergency room experience, and you reacted to that. So, were you reacting to the sight of a bee on a red rose, or were you back in the emergency room, struggling to breathe, getting a shot, and waiting until your body's reaction eased? Actually, the answer is yes and "yes". You were reacting to both. You were acting on the emotions that lurked in the shadow of your childhood experience.

You see, all of our memories contain all of the senses -- sight, sound, taste, smell and touch. They also contain the emotions you felt at the time the memory was made. Each of these goes to a different segment of the brain; so, for a memory to return, the brain must gather all the elements from the various storage areas for each of the senses plus the emotions and put them together to form a complete picture.

Human beings live in the present and in the past. Those who do not choose to recover from the negative events of the past are bound to repeat them and live their everyday lives based on those experiences. We may attempt to forget what happened in the past, but, since the mind is programmed to remember, the harder we try to forget the more we remember. We can ignore, we can vehemently refuse to review or revisit or we can deny the past, but the contents of that filing cabinet, even what's in the locked drawers lurking in the shadows, can ooze out to haunt us and cause us to wound others. The past is a reference point, and the future is a goal. We use the past and the present to plan the future. Without the past present in our experience, it becomes difficult to formulate or dream of the future. Even past negative experiences are helpful, in that they teach us to steer clear of negative stimuli, but we must choose to not allow them to dictate our every action.

Amazing, isn't it, how the human brain and the mind are so precisely and perfectly made? Neuron (brain cell) connects with neuron forming a pathway, a chain of neurons. Repeatedly experienced, a habit is soon formed and sometimes, even without premeditation, without thinking about it, a pattern of behaving or a way of thinking is formed and "set in cement," so to speak. However, whether positive or negative, habits can be broken or positively changed.

According to Dr. Bruce Perry, a neuro-psychiatrist and former professor at Baylor University, habits can be changed:

> " . . . *because the human brain is very plastic, meaning that it is capable of changing in response to patterned, repetitive activation. Reading, hearing a new language, and learning a different motor skill such as typing, are all examples of the brain's plasticity in action. But not all parts of the brain are equally plastic.*
>
> *The malleability (mold-ability) of specific human brain areas is different. The most complex areas of the brain – the cortex – is the most plastic. We can modify some cortex-related functions throughout life with minimal effort. For example, even a 90-year-old person can learn a new phone number.*
>
> *The lower parts of the brain, which mediate (referee) core regulatory functions, are not very plastic. And that is for good reason. It would be very destructive for these basic and life-sustaining functions to*

be easily modified by experience once they were organized. A lesion that kills one million neurons in the cortex can be overcome. For instance, people recover language and motor skills following a stroke. Conversely, a lesion in the brainstem that killed as many cells would result in death.

The degree of plasticity is related to two main factors: the stage of development and the area or system of the brain. Once an area of the brain is organized, it is much less responsive to the environment, or plastic. A critical concept related to memory and brain plasticity is the differential plasticity of various brain systems."

(Perry, Bruce. "The Amazing Brain and Human Development, Lesson 2." http://www.childtrauma.com)

You may think of yourself as worthless. You may have formed the habit of becoming easily angered with the slightest provocation, or you may face every experience of life with fear. But you can change. You do not have to remain the product of your past and the shadow that follows you! The change requires personal knowledge about your history, a willingness to face what seems very difficult to focus upon because of its detrimental effects on you as a child, the willingness to look at how what happened still affects you today and an agreement to allow healing and forgiveness to come to you through positive actions you take.

The one newly discovered thing that is so encouraging is that the brain does not stop changing.

In other words, its capacity for change does not cease until death, unless there is an illness which sabotages that capability. Regardless of age, if you are teachable, if you are willing to learn, you are fixable. Old habits may die hard, as the old saying goes, but they can die! Your shadows can shorten and diminish.

Chapter Three

Rejection in the Womb

". . . the unborn child is a feeling, remembering, aware being, and because he is, what happens to him – what happens to all of us – in the nine months between conception and birth molds and shapes personality, drives and ambitions in very important ways."

Verny, Thomas. The Secret Life of the Unborn Child. (15)

According to Dr. John Bowlby, the father of Attachment Theory and a former researcher at the Tavistock Institute in London:

> *"Maternal deprivation is a state of affairs in which the child lacks that warm, intimate and continuous relationship with his mother (or permanent mother- substitute) in which both find satisfaction and enjoyment."*
>
> Maternal Care and Mental Health

Are you one of the many whose conception came at a time inconvenient for your parents? Did they tell you that you were a mistake, a surprise, that they didn't want any more children or that you were born the wrong sex to suit them? If you are, just endeavor to understand that this was their problem, their issue. That you had to suffer as a result was also their issue, which they transferred to you. You do not have to carry that burden any longer. You can give it back to them, even if they are deceased, and can come to realize that there is a divine plan for your existence. Then you should do your best to discover it and fulfill the plan, thus achieving satisfaction and joy! The shadow containing their words can be eliminated.

Remember the movie, "Simon Birch?" Perhaps if you haven't seen it, you should rent it and watch it with a friend In this film, a midget finally discovers that he too has a purpose – a mighty purpose – and finds himself fulfilling it. Amazing how novels (A Prayer for Owen Meany by John Irving) can come up with stories that illustrate a powerful point. In this one film, the point is that every person has a reason for living; there is a plan for each of us, and, regardless of our parents' acceptance or rejection of us, our life still does have value. If you have seen the film, which one of the characters is most like you? Why?

Maybe this is true of you -- there you are floating in the womb, needing to connect with your mother, but she does not respond to you. The circumstances that render her unable to connect may stem from her own personal history or from the situation in which she finds herself during her pregnancy. It could be that her angst is so great that her adrenal glands are producing large amounts of the stress hormones, called catecholamines: adrenaline, nor-adrenaline and cortisol. It is helpful to understand that the connections between the brain's neurons are **negatively** impacted when a pregnant mother is stressed. Stress hormones are sent to the fetus via the umbilical cord, and abnormal connections may form between the neurons in the brain of the child. In addition, these hormones cause the fetus to become agitated and anxious, and even cause an elevated pulse rate.

After studying and following 2000 women, Dr. Minika Lukesch, a psychologist at Constantine University in Frankfurt, Germany, concluded that the mother's attitude had the greatest single impact on how the child turned out. The children of accepting mothers turned out to be much healthier, emotionally and physically, than those of rejecting mothers. Evidence shows and we concur that our wounds commence while we are still in our formation process. (Verny, 47-48)

Modern science has much to say about the development of the child in the womb, and about the impact of the environment upon that child. In the 1960's, science discovered a post-birth system of connecting and communication called "bonding" and since then we have determined that bonding begins while the child is in the womb rather than after birth. The child is affected by the hormones from the mother's body, and the hormone levels are influenced by the mother's state of being. It has also been determined that the father has a profound influence on the child through his relationship with the pregnant mother. If the parents' relationship is a loving and supportive one, the mother will feel loved and supported and those feelings will be sent to the child. Conversely, if the mother is stressed due to a poor or abusive relationship with the father, the fetus in the womb will receive a bolus of stress hormones, negatively impacting his or her development.

Time Magazine's October, 2010 article reports further:

> *"Studies have suggested that women who are pregnant during historical periods of stress or famine give birth to offspring who are more likely than those born in calmer*

> *times to develop schizophrenia in young adulthood. Maternal malnutrition may disrupt neural development, contributing to the illness." Regarding depression, the article states: "Research has found increased rates of premature delivery and low birth weight among babies born to depressed women. Scientists are also discovering possible links between a mother's mood and a fetus's sensitivity to stress, and perhaps even the temperament it exhibits after birth."*

In an article published in 1977 in *New Society,* Dr. Dennis Stott rates a bad marriage or relationship as among the greatest causes of emotional and physical damage. He states that a woman in a bad marriage has a 237% greater risk of producing a psychologically or physically damaged child: they are five times more fearful and jumpy, and by age 4 or 5, undersized, timid and emotionally dependent on the mother to an inordinate degree. They become predisposed to suspiciousness, distrust and introversion. For them, relating to others and self-assertion will be difficult. (Children in the Womb: The Effects of Stress, published in New Society, magazine) page 77,

These ideas about fetal development and parental influence upon it come from laboratories in America, Canada, England, France, Sweden, Germany, Austria, New Zealand and Switzerland, where, for several decades, scientists have been quietly developing a whole new view of the fetus, of birth and of the beginning of life.

Millions of neurons (brain cells) are formed early in fetal development, and their connection one with another commences as pregnancy continues. By twenty-eight weeks of gestation, there are 124 million connections between neurons. A newborn has approximately 253 million connections, and by eight months of age 572 million connections have been made. This rate of new connections begins to slow in number toward the end of the first year of life.

Each neuron has an axon and numerous dendrites. These connect with each other and begin to form a network of wiring that looks as complicated as the electrical wiring for a city as large as New York. Thoughts and actions cause activity in the brain with neuronal connections firing like fireworks on the fourth of July. As each new ability is gained and each new thought or feeling experienced, new connections are made with older ones, thus creating the ability to remember the past, experience the present and contemplate or plan the future. It is amazing how perfectly planned and precisely orchestrated the development of a new human being is, especially in the first months of fetal and infant life.

Dr. Thomas Verny reports that a child's ego (the sum of what we think and feel about ourselves: our strengths, drives, desires, vulnerabilities and insecurities) is formed between the fifth and sixth months of gestation, when the ability to remember and feel is in place. (63)

The brain's capacity is astounding. With approximately 100 billion neurons functioning in the adult brain, each neuron has the capability of holding as much information as the entire set of the Encyclopedia Britannica. Imagine all of that capacity for knowing and thinking in a three pound brain – an entire universe in such a small mass.

Dr. Thomas Verny's conclusions are that what affects a child does so directly. That is why maternal emotions etch themselves so deeply in his psyche and why their tug remains so powerful late in life.

A study by Dr. Michael Liberman shows that anxiety (quickening of the heartbeat) is shown in the unborn when his mother simply thinks about smoking a cigarette. The child has no way of knowing that the mother is smoking, only that his oxygen supply is diminished through the placental blood periodically. Psychologically speaking, this produces a chronic state of uncertainty and fear, which predisposes the child to a deep-seated, conditioned anxiety. (20)

A team of researchers at Columbia University, studied and discovered that famine or poor nutrition in the first few months of pregnancy will produce a strong tendency to being overweight in adulthood. This early starvation of the fetus could easily be interpreted by the child as being a display of rejection, even though the child is without language to actually think. Is the fetus capable of understanding or labeling felt experiences as rejection? Absolutely not. During the fetal stages of development, the ability to label a physical feeling is not in place. A child has to understand word meanings for the labeling process to occur. That happens later in childhood development, but the cellular memories exist, nonetheless. Feelings arrive before thinking and feelings precipitate thoughts later in life. The child would feel and later think, "If you won't feed me, you must not love me."

Some adults share that they were in the womb when their mothers attempted to abort them. Hot baths, the insertion of objects into the mother's vagina, jumping from high places and many other methods have been used in an attempt to destroy the developing child. Abortion clinics abound where the procedures are successful. Many have survived their mother's endeavor to destroy them, yet each have a price to pay in their later feelings of rejection.

A national survey was conducted in 1977 among grammar school students by Temple University's Institute for Survey Research. Of a total sample of 2,208 children, nearly one in seven was, by admission of the parents, a consciously unwanted pregnancy. These unwanted children were found to be in poorer health, to have more learning problems, and to be more prone to accidents or injuries than were planned-pregnancy children. In 1995, the National Survey for Family Growth compiled these 1994 statistics: 49% of 1000 pregnancies were unintended. 54% of those unintended pregnancies were aborted. Evoy, (22)

Whether the rejection was as blatant as an abortion attempt or more subtle like not wanting a child and wishing it away, still the scars remain. Usually if a child was not wanted during pregnancy, there will be remaining elements of rejecting the child after his/ her birth. Many parents actually say the words: "you never should have been born!", and many children, upon hearing those words, have fact added to the feelings of rejection they already possess. Those words loom in the shadows and peek out, often interrupting or sabotaging success in any arena.

Dr. Carlos Garelli from the University of Buenos Aires Child Development Department believes that rejection is the main cause of criminal behavior later in life. In our 2003 visit to the Tennessee State Penitentiary – Maximum Security and Death Row Division, approximately forty inmates attended a mini-seminar we conducted there. As we began to speak about rejection and told Ron's experience with it, one man after another jumped to his feet to tell the story of his own rejection. Many shared that at a certain point in their lives, usually in the teen years they decided to take charge of their lives, striking out at those who rejected them and at others as well.

Regardless of when your initial rejection occurred, you are fixable. Knowledge is power, and the more you can learn about rejection and how it has affected you, the faster you can choose to overcome its devastating results.

Chapter Four

Rejection – What Is It?

Most people know that certain vital things are necessary in order to keep a human body alive. Food, water, shelter and human interaction are but a few of the ingredients that will insure the physical well-being of a child. However, having those needs fulfilled will not guarantee emotional maturity or stability. It may not even insure that the child will do well physically.

What is rejection? It is a refusal to accept or acknowledge. To reject means to discard, push aside or discount. It is a refusal to accept, to hear, to touch or to consider important. Now with all of these definitions, do you *feel* that you were rejected? If so when? Was it when your mother discovered she was pregnant? Was it when you were born and were not the gender she hoped for? Was your birth unplanned and were you told that you were an accident? Or was it just a feeling you got, even though your needs for food, water, shelter and clothing may have been met?

In his book, The Rejected, Dr. John Joseph Evoy, then a professor emeritus at Gonzaga University in Spokane, Washington and an expert in this subject, says that his clients described rejection as:

> *". . . their emotionally toned knowledge that they were not loved and wanted for themselves – by one or both parents."* (14)

In his clinical practice, Dr. Evoy would see only clients who reported that rejection was their issue, and after thirty-two years of working with these men and women, Dr. Evoy knew them and their trauma inside and out. He says that very few of his patients entertained any serious doubts about whether they had been rejected, and they were able to identify the degree to which they felt rejected, even if they couldn't actually put a finger on the causative element..

He states:

> *"A closely related consideration here is that there is a great deal of evidence to show that little children normally see their parents as ten-feet-high giants who are both omniscient (all knowing) and omnipotent (all powerful). Accordingly, almost without exception, small children do not question the correctness of perceived parental evaluations and attitudes toward them, no matter how much they might dislike, resent, or be hurt by them. This correctness exists both at the child's intellectual and emotional levels."* (15)

So you see, if Mommy and Daddy say it, and act as though they mean it, it **is** true, as far as a child is concerned. Comments like, "You should never have been born," "We didn't want you," "You should've been a boy," or "You're dumb and stupid" are taken at face value by the child and for sure, these are messages of rejection.

According to Evoy and his patients, rejection was not something that they happened to feel when they were depressed or otherwise "out of sorts" and then it later disappeared when their spirits picked up.

Rather, once they openly recognized that painful feeling and labeled it appropriately, it remained constant for them. Even when they were not aware of the feeling, it did not disappear; it was just on the periphery of their awareness. (15) It was the shadow that followed them.

These rejected clients of Dr. Evoy said that their parents expressed rejection by what they did or said or by exaggerated neglect of and indifference toward them. It was a prolonged disinterest or lack of concern about what happened to them. Those parents who more actively rejected them did so in their actions of abuse, which contained the parent's feelings that they did not love or want the children for who they were themselves.

Through his years of research, Dr. Evoy's findings agree with several other psychologists, that the rejected would *"rather choose an active expression of rejection as being emotionally less painful. They chose to have their parents hurt them rather than ignore them."*

In Dr. Alice Miller's book, "*The Drama of Being a Child,* we learn:

- *"The child has a primary need from the very beginning of her life to be regarded and respected as the person she really is at any given time.*
- *When we speak here of "the person she really is at any given time", we mean emotions, sensations and their expression from the first day onward.*
- *In an atmosphere of respect and tolerance for her feelings, the child, in the phase of separation, will be able to give up symbiosis*

with the mother and accomplish the steps toward individuation and autonomy.

- *If they are to furnish these prerequisites for the healthy development of their child, the parents themselves ought to have grown up in such an atmosphere. If they did, they will be able to assure the child the protection and well-being she needs to develop trust.*
- *Parents who did not experience this climate themselves as children are themselves deprived; throughout their lives they will continue to look for what their own parents could not give them at the appropriate time – the presence of a person who is completely aware of them and takes them seriously.*
- *This search, of course can never fully succeed since it relates to a situation that belongs irrevocably to the past, namely to the time right after birth and during early childhood.*
- *A person with this unsatisfied and unconscious (because repressed) need will nevertheless be compelled to attempt its gratification through substitute means, as long as she ignores her repressed life history.*
- *The most efficacious objects for substitute gratification are a parent's own children. The newborn baby or small child is completely dependent on his parents, and since their caring is essential for his existence, he does all he can to avoid losing them. From the very first day onward, he will muster all his resources to that end, like a small plant that turns toward the sun in order to survive.(7-8)*

What an insightful commentary, don't you think? The way Dr. Miller explains her point is so logical in its progression. Basically, she states simply that if Mother and Father were wounded in their character-forming years chances are good that their children will also be wounded by them. We pass on what we know to our children, and they suffer the consequences of generations of wounding by parents, grandparents, great-grandparents etc., as far back as the beginning of time.

Alice Miller was herself a wounded child who finally came to acknowledge, accept and heal from her childhood pain in her sixties. This world-famous and well-written psychoanalyst chose to give up her membership in the American Psychological Association when, at a convention in 1995, they determined that since sexual abuse of children is so common an occurrence that it might be okay. In disgust, she relinquished her membership and chose to continue her work by writing books that would "tell the truth" regarding the devastating effects of child abuse of any kind.

In her book, Banished Knowledge Dr. Miller states:

> *"When a child must consume all her capability and energy for the required labor of repression (the putting away from the conscious mind, memories that are too painful to retain); when, in addition, she has never known what it is to be loved and protected by someone, this child will eventually also be incapable of protecting herself and organizing her life in a meaningful and productive manner. This child will continue to torment herself in destructive*

relationships, taking up with irresponsible partners and suffering from them; but she is unlikely to be able to grasp that the origin of all this suffering is to be found in her own parents and others involved in her upbringing. That former labor of repression to ensure survival renders such an insight impossible, contrary now to the interests of the adult who was once that child. If to survive, a child is required to ignore certain things, the chances are that she will be required to continue to ignore those things for the rest of her life. The life-saving function of repression in childhood is transformed in adulthood into a life-destroying force."

Is Dr. Miller saying here that a rejected child cannot recover from those early wounds? Not at all! She is saying that, without intervention, she will continue to live in similar circumstances to those of her childhood. This has become her norm; it's what she has become used to. She considers her worth and value to be either the enduring of trauma and violence or being totally ignored in a relationship.

What is difficult in these circumstances is that the girl-become-woman blames her current partner or life circumstances for what she is suffering, rather than being able to identify the true source of her angst. The partner gets the blame for what the parents have done or neglected to do, while the woman herself refuses responsibility. Since she is the product of the parent, blaming the parent is to share in that responsibility. This may not be a conscious thought process, but a subconscious force determining behaviors. Suffering the blame personally is a load far too heavy to bear.

Many whose trauma in childhood has been grave, will be determined to not remain the product of wounding, but to become the one *doing* the wounding. This is one of the reasons that our prisons are filled with such angry men and women. They have been tortured by rejection and other abuses in their early childhood, and at some point in life, have decided to turn the tables.

George is a perfect example of this. The youngest of three children, the only boy and a redhead as well, George became the "scapegoat" for the family very early on. He was blamed for everything that went wrong in the family, including the misdeeds of his older sisters or younger siblings. He was regularly beaten in the cellar's furnace room with oak yardsticks and then a wide leather strap. Many nights he would go to bed bleeding and blistered from the beating he had just received. Dad did the dastardly deeds, but his Mother sat on the cellar steps egging Daddy on to beat him harder and longer over things for which he had already suffered beatings.

On his twelfth birthday, he was called out to the garage, and there in a wooden crate was his wished for bicycle. Thrilled and delighted he jumped up and down with glee, until his father told him that the bike was going to be returned to the store for something the boy supposedly had done wrong the previous day. George said in his later years, that it was on that day he decided that he would allow no one to get close to him again so that he would not suffer again as he was suffering that day. He decided that he would take what he wanted and be the cause of pain to others rather than the recipient of it.

Unfortunately, the rest of George's life told the story of his childhood. In and out of relationships and in and out of prison, he remained emotionally distant and took what he wanted, disregarding the consequences to others, especially those in his family. He was destined to die a lonely man and a pauper. None of his family attended his memorial service; only those who lived in the same senior housing complex as he cared enough to see that he had a "proper burial." During the last two years of his life, however, George acquired knowledge about human behaviors, acknowledged his own painful childhood and made noticeable behavioral changes. Unfortunately only Ron and the folks where he lived got to observe the new man.

Psychiatrist E.F. Vogel studied the marriages of parents who had emotionally disturbed children. In an article he published in the journal *"Psychiatry,"* he states that one of the determinants in the development of emotionally disturbed children appeared to be that the children were being used as a means of preserving their parents' marriage. A common denominator in this particular study was that the children felt that they were not wanted for themselves, but for saving the marriage of their parents. The way the child felt about this self-seeking behavior of their parents was the determining factor in their emotional disturbance.

Many children report that fulfilling their parents' unmet longings became their mandate in life. In order to get acceptance and love from parents, they had to fulfill their mother and/or father's unmet longings. Such things as good grades in school, musical accomplishments, certain careers or specific life partners were demanded in order for the child to be considered successful, and therefore, accepted by the parent. The child comes to believe that if he or she is not "successful" he will not be loved by the parent. Others felt that unless they met all of their parents' expectations, they would be disappointing or letting down their parents. This engenders a life of fear: fear of failure and fear of disappointing others.

Very common, especially among strictly religious families, is the concept that to be loved and accepted by God, one has to work to earn this acceptance. Such seemingly mild statements as "be a good boy," puts a child in a predicament of remembering and fulfilling all of the rules in order to be loved and accepted – by parents and by God. This does, of course, include refraining from any behaviors that are forbidden by the parents, the school, the church or society, and therefore places the child "on guard" or anxious about even the possibility of breaking a rule.

Some children have to closely monitor their behaviors and their parents' reactions to them, to find ones that will get him or her love and acceptance. Add to this responsibility that of trying to "make a parent happy" by playing a certain role in the family, and you have confusion and too heavy a weight for a child to carry. Some have to actually play the role of the opposite gender in order to make Mommy or Daddy happy or to gain some amount of adulation.

World Wide Evidence

Over forty-five years of research into parental acceptance and rejection has been conducted by Ronald P. Rohner, Ph.D. A leading expert on multi-cultural parental acceptance/rejection and its effect upon the offspring, he is the founder of the University of Connecticut's **Ronald and Nancy Rohner Center for the Study of Parental Acceptance and Rejection** and the author of several books and numerous articles on this subject. Dr. Rohner calls upon nearly 2000 studies in every major ethnic group in the United States, and several hundred societies worldwide, to report the implications and results of rejection upon children and upon adults who were rejected in childhood.

From an article compiled by several of the center's staff, which reports multiple research projects, come five conclusions. The paper itself is prepared for academia, but the five conclusions can easily be understood:

"Nearly 200 studies suggest that children's feelings of being loved, cared about, wanted and appreciated probably have greater developmental consequences than any other single parental influence. Improved messages of parental love appear to be the most salient (significant) route through which effective parenting techniques contribute to healthy child development."

1. Extensive study in every major ethnic group within the U.S. and in several hundred societies worldwide reveals a common meaning structure that children use to determine if they are loved (accepted). Culture and ethnicity shape the specific words and behaviors that carry these concepts, but children everywhere seem to organize their perceptions around these dimensions of parenting:
    - Warmth and affection
    - Hostility and aggression
    - Indifference and neglect
    - Undifferentiated rejection (cannot be observed by others, but is felt by child)

Every cultural and ethnic group has ways to communicate love, and children readily recognize these ways."

2. "Compared to children who feel loved, children who feel rejected are at greater risk for developing specific forms of psychological maladjustment. In turn, these feelings and behaviors often become associated everywhere with:
    - Behavior problems, conduct disorders, delinquency, and perhaps adult criminality
    - Depression and depressed affects
    - Substance (drug and alcohol) abuse-among other problems"
3. "The vast majority of studies testing the major postulates of PARTheory's (Parental Acceptance/Rejection Theory) Personality Sub-theory, show that children who experience themselves to be rejected also display a constellation of personality dispositions – a syndrome.
    - Hostility
    - Aggression
    - Passive-Aggression
    - Emotional unresponsiveness,
    - Immature dependence or defensive independence.
    - Impaired self-esteem
    - Impaired self-adequacy
    - Emotional Instability
    - Negative Worldview"

4. "Evidence from PARTheory research documents the fact that fathers' love-related behaviors often have as strong or even stronger implications for children's social-emotional development than do mothers' love-related behaviors. For example, fathers' love-related behavior (or the love-related behavior of the other significant male caregivers) is often as strongly – or more so – associated with offspring's sense of health and well-being in childhood and later adulthood, as mother's. Paternal (fathers') rejection, however, is sometimes more strongly associated than mothers' rejection with such negative developmental outcomes as depression and depressive affect, conduct problems and substance abuse, to mention but three outcomes."

   (Rohner, Khaleque and Cournoyer) For a review of the entire document, refer to Center for the Study of Parental Acceptance and Rejection at the University of Connecticut.

Simply Stated:

1. Being loved, cared about, wanted and accepted is the single most important factor in the development of healthy children.
2. In every culture children recognize whether or not they are loved and accepted by the same means: warmth and affection, hostility and aggression, indifference and neglect or undifferentiated rejection.
3. Children who are rejected are at a greater risk for psychological maladjustment.
4. Children who feel rejected display negative personality behaviors.

5. Fathers' love-related behaviors have as strong or even stronger influence on children than do mother's love-related behaviors.

Rejection is real, loitering in the shadows it is a nightmare! For the ones who felt it in childhood, it is a way of thinking, feeling and predicting the outcome of all relationships in the future. Rejected people look for rejection everywhere, and if they don't find it, they manufacture it in their minds or display behaviors guaranteed to get them rejected, because rejection feels normal to them.

If you are a victim or you are in an intimate relationship with a rejected individual, you know that enough is never enough. Nobody gets it completely right for the rejected. "I think that you love me, but." These are frequently heard words by those who love the rejected.

And – there's hope. The rejected can heal from the confinement of their mind – the destructive shadow that torments. There is a way to coax the old wounds out of the shadows and a key to set them free. Understanding the prison they are in is the first step out of that dreadful and lonely imprisonment.

Now, let's look at some of the occurrences of life that cause one to experience rejection.

Chapter Five

What's the Set-Up?

It all begins in the womb – **that** news you have already discovered. Now we are going to examine how our earliest experiences can set us up for feelings later in life of having been rejected or traumatized when we were children. We sense that something isn't right with us, and we don't understand the origins of those feelings. Rejection can be quite insidious and is usually unrecognized or labeled as such until later years.

A Difficult or Forceps Delivery: Evidence now abounds regarding the effects of birth traumas on both the physical and the psychological or emotional aspects of later life.

An October 1987 report listed in Thomas Verny's book, *The Secret Life of the Unborn Child,* from the State Institute of Forensic Medicine in Stockholm, Solna, Sweden, states:

> *"The study was undertaken to test whether obstetric procedures are of importance for eventual adult behavior of the newborn, as ecological data from the United States seem to indicate. Birth record data was gathered for 412 forensic victims comprising suicides, alcoholics and drug addicts born in Stockholm after 1940, and who died there in 1978-1984. The births of the victims were unevenly distributed among six hospitals.*

> *Comparison with 2,901 controls, and mutual comparison of categories, showed that suicides involving asphyxiation were closely associated with asphyxia at birth, suicides by violent mechanical means were associated with mechanical birth trauma and drug addiction was associated with opiate and/or barbiturate administration to mothers during labor. Irrespective of the mechanism transferring the birth imprinting---the results show that obstetric procedures should be carefully evaluated and possibly modified to prevent eventual self-destructive behavior."*
>
> Reported in *Pre-Parenting* by Verny

Of course, we are aware that emergencies occur just prior to and during birth, and, in those cases, often dramatic measures are necessary to preserve the life of the child and/or the mother. This is understandable, but what do we do to minimize the results to the child caused by these events? Extensive time with the child by birth parents, warmth and affection and the reassuring words that the child is OK, help in the hours, days and weeks, yes, even years, after the traumatic delivery.

A difficult delivery causes stress to the mother, which, if the child is still in the womb, will transfer to the child. In the birthing process, if a child is not progressing through the birth canal, turned the wrong way for easy delivery, has the umbilical cord wrapped around its neck or is in distress (causing heart rate to elevate or depress) this creates stress in the child which raises levels of cortisol and adrenaline in its body. These hormones received in large amounts can cause abnormal connections between the neurons in the child's brain. A child delivered with the use of forceps endures pressure to both sides of the head. As you know, the skull is still pliable in a newborn so pressure would be received by the brain housed inside the skull, and stretching of the neck to pull the child out of the birth canal.

In addition, it appears that mothers who experience other complications in pregnancy such as toxemia (blood pressure increased to a dangerous level) may birth a child who has emotional wounds from her illness. One mother told us that her eight year old daughter, who endured several months of hospitalization while still in-utero due to her mother's toxemia, had always been an angry child. At one point in her eighth year, she took a butcher knife from the kitchen and, in a rage, thrust the point to her mother's throat, screaming, "I wanna' kill you!" Of course the mother was devastated by her daughter's actions. When asked about the family situation, the mother reported that there was no provocation due to stress in the home, but that the child had always been angry and directed that anger mostly at her mother.

When a mother's blood pressure increases, the child in the womb will receive less oxygen, thus producing the feeling of suffocating. Since that was this child's experience most of her in-utero life, it seems logical that her mother would be the object of her angst.

Wrong Sex / Unwanted Child / Adopted Child: How would you feel if your mother or father told you that they wanted a child of the opposite sex than what you are? "We had a name picked out for a boy 'cause that's what we wanted, so when we got you instead, we just gave you a boy's name."

Take for example the woman in her 70's, who said that her real name was Stephen. We thought for sure that she meant Stephanie, but she quickly informed us that her parents wanted a ninth son. They were planning on calling him Stephen, so, when she was born a girl, they just called her the desired son's name. She went on to say that she was never allowed to eat at the table with her parents and siblings because she was a girl. She ate alone in the pantry. Mother had "earned her way to the table by producing nine boys," she added. She was the outcast, the slave, the unwanted and unaccepted child. Was it any wonder that she was a very unhappy woman? Rejection does not create happiness!

Many children have been told that they never should have been born. "You're an accident," they are told by thoughtless parents who conceived their little one at an inconvenient time or out of the bonds of marriage. These children wonder why they should continue living if the parents who created them didn't want them.

The adopted child always wonders WHY birth mother and father "gave me away." "Why didn't they want me? What was wrong with me?" The child may have been adopted by the best possible parents, but the question lingers until from the mouth of one of the birth parents, the whole story is told. One young man said that his adoptive parents had been so wonderful that he thought that he would never want to meet his birth parents. However, one day, seeing himself in the mirror as he shaved, the thought came to him – "I wonder if there's anyone in the world who I look like." That began his quest to see his father. They met once. He said that when he spotted his father he knew instantly that this was the man. A meeting and a lunch later, his questions answered, the young man was satisfied and has not needed further contact with his birth parent.

A Late-in-Life Baby or Child Expected to Fix the Parent's Marriage: It has been said by many, that God was wise when He gave babies and little kids to young mothers. The young have the energy to play with and spend time with their children, while older mothers have, in most cases, less energy and thus a harder time keeping up with all of the demands of the children. Many years have passed and many world changes have taken place since the parents were kids. Keeping up with these changes and understanding the wants of the children isn't easy for older parents.

A child expected to repair the parents' marriage, carries a heavy burden, indeed. They are able to pick up the attitudes of the parents and the heavy responsibility they carry to be the glue that holds their parents together. Many parents actually think that their marriage difficulties will magically disappear with the arrival of a newborn they have created, but all they end up with is another complication to their already strained relationship.

Often in the home where Mother and Dad are not getting along well with each other, the daughter becomes the father's confidant or the son becomes the mother's. The child is then given adult responsibilities and, unfortunately, is most often a failure in performing them. There are other negative consequences to this dynamic also, but we'll save those for later.

Premature Birth – Birth Defect (Real or Perceived): Expelled from the womb far too soon, a premature baby is just not ready for the world and its demands. Delicate, tiny, possibly unable to breathe well on its own, and usually without the warmth and nurturing of parents, these little ones suffer lack of bonding, with effects that last a lifetime. Add to this the passive experience of a crisis in mother's pregnancy, the baby in distress in the womb, the rush to the operating room for a cesarean birth, and fear then complicates the thoughts and feelings of the child. Dr. Thomas Verny states in his book, Pre-Parenting:

> *"Obstetricians agree that of all the birth scenarios, the most devastating is prematurity. The typical period of gestation is 40 weeks, but 6-8 percent of babies are born at 38 weeks or less. Though medical science has made progress in recent years in increasing life expectancy for preemies, those who survive frequently suffer breathing difficulties, cerebral palsy, intellectual handicaps, and other problems."* (80)

What of the effect of an incubator and a Neonatal Intensive Care Unit? These tiny ones are subjected to frequent tests and the absence of the warmth and affection of their mothers, the ones with whom they must connect.

We could go on and on citing stories and giving alarming statistics, but would rather suggest to those interested, that you borrow from the library or order Dr. Verny's excellent book: *Pre-parenting* from www.yourLRI.com.

Not Bonding at Birth: The first two to three hours of life are designed for the newborn to connect emotionally with his mother and father using all of his senses. Unfortunately, often the circumstances of delivery, hospital traditions and the health of mother or newborn do not allow for this time for the three of them to be alone to discover each other.

There is a "window of opportunity that allows for this discovery during these first hours. The eyesight of the newborn is clear with a focal length of 15-18 inches, the distance from the mother's arms to her face. Finally, baby gets to actually see this person in whose body he or she has been growing for nine months. He gets to smell the familiar smell of her body, hear her familiar voice, touch the soft and welcoming body and taste the colostrum she provides at her breast for those first hours of life. This is the ideal – God's original plan.

However, all too often those first hours are spent apart from mother in a nursery where routine procedures are performed or perhaps life-saving procedures are conducted. In addition, Mother may have been anesthetized for the birth and is not capable of holding and bonding with her child. The routine procedures of nurses and doctors all too often preclude the wishes of the parents or the best interest of the baby. In past years we have thought it vital to weigh the newborn, measure his length, take blood tests, put drops in baby's eyes, clothe him in a little shirt and diaper and tightly wrap the newborn in a receiving blanket. In most cases, these measures are not necessary, but are the hospital's routine and, thus, are imposed upon the family. Today, more gentle methods of treating a newborn and allowances for time immediately following birth with mother and father are allowed and encouraged in many hospitals and birthing centers.

Father Not in Delivery or Father Not Actively Involved With the Child: Every child needs a mother and a father; this has been proven through the years, and was God's plan in the first place. Unfortunately in our society, fathers are frequently absent from the home due to divorce, separation, war or work which takes him away. It is also true that many fathers have the idea that caring for baby is a mother's work, and he should not be involved. Remember, we learn from our character-forming years, and if the father did not have a present and involved dad in his childhood, he will not know how to be a father to his own child without instruction and learning.

A few years ago, a little girl was born to a young couple who thought that they could not have children. Her conception was the result of very pricey in vitro-fertilization. As the time for delivery approached, the husband and the wife's mother were both in the delivery room at the wife's request. Suddenly, both Mother and baby went into distress, and emergency procedures were required. Grandma feared losing both her daughter and her grandchild. After several unsuccessful attempts to instill an epidural, the mother was in agony from the pain of the spinal injections and the contractions, and frightened at the prospect of losing her child.

Grandma had been well educated about what a newborn needs, so finally she begged, "Just knock her out and get that baby born!" The doctor listened, and finally the longed-for baby girl was born, pink and healthy. The nurses were about to take her from the delivery room when Grandma spoke up again.

"Oh no you don't! You give that baby to her Daddy!" Again, the staff complied with Grandma's demands, and the little girl was placed in Daddy's arms. There he spoke quiet words of love and comfort to her, and the two bonded. She had heard his voice from inside the womb for nine months, and now she got to add the face to the voice. Later Grandma was given her newborn granddaughter, and for quite a long period, she talked to her little one, sang to her and spoke words of love and adoration.

Was this a successful beginning for the little girl? Absolutely. Of course, the upshot is that Daddy is number one in this little girl's affections, and Grandma is treasured. Fathers are necessary. Fathers are important. Ask yourself how present and powerful your father was in your life. If he was absent how has it has impacted you?

Child Born Out of Wedlock: Single parents abound in this day and age. Young girls, perhaps still in high school, find themselves pregnant by a boyfriend or "just some guy" who enjoyed himself at her expense while she was intoxicated or drugged, or perhaps compliant. It's quite likely that the two decided to "enjoy" themselves thinking that no one will get hurt. Maybe the pregnancy occurred for a couple who planned to marry, or weren't quite sure yet, but were sexually active.

In many cases, these couples marry thinking that it is the right thing to do, since they have created a child, but they were not mature enough for the responsibilities and the compromises necessary in a marriage. Often the wife wonders after the vows are said, if the husband married her out of real love for her or because he felt forced to do so. This weighs heavy upon them both. The wife's tendency will be to make her husband "prove" his love. He may not have really loved her, but feeling "trapped," he chose to marry and raise his child. Theirs will no doubt be a difficult or short-lived marriage.

What of the situations where the sperm donor does not want to marry the pregnant girl? Alone she must decide what to do. "Shall I abort the child? Shall I carry and deliver and then give my child for adoption? Shall I deliver the child and attempt to support and raise him alone? Will my parents help me while I finish school or work? Who will end up being the child's mother – me or my mother?" Many young girls say that they actually want to have a baby, even though not married, so that they will have someone to love them. In this situation, the baby is responsible for loving the loveless mother – the roles are reversed. Instead of mother supplying what the child needs, the mother steals love from the relationship with the child.

Again, we end up with the situation in which the child soon wonders who and where the father is, why they were abandoned by the father, and they feel that they are an inconvenience. For this and other reasons, sexual union should be saved for after the commitment of marriage.

Child Called Names Perceived as Negative by the Child: "You are dumb!", "Idiot!", "Worthless!" and many other such expressions are used by far too many parents and caregivers and are directed at little ones whose characters are still in their formation process. In early childhood, little ones believe what they hear from parents or other primary caregivers, so when a child is emotionally abused by words or by silence, the child believes that his worth and value is exactly what the parent has verbalized or left unsaid.

A human being is a success or a failure based on his personal view of his value. Emotionally abused children are seldom successful in later life unless through intervention by another person who does see value in them, or through professional counseling, their self worth can be raised. On the other hand, some do their best to excel either academically, in their career or through hard work in an attempt to prove worth and value.

Were you given a nickname that you didn't like as a kid or one that was a derogatory term? Even that nickname heard over and over again can steal a sense of self-confidence from you. Remember, these names may have been directed at you, but look back at those who said them for a moment. Do you honestly believe that the ones who said them had a valid sense of their own worth? Usually, those who call others derogatory and hurtful names are really directing those names, unknowingly, at themselves.

Fighting Between Parents and/or Communication Lacking in the Family: The pendulum of domestic unrest and difficulty swings from one extreme to the other. Partners either give each other "the silent treatment" or, in cases of domestic violence, there is outright war. Children observe their parents fighting about trivial matters such as the direction the toilet paper should roll or major concerns such as finances, infidelity or discipline of the children. Crouched behind the living room sofa, a four-year-old son watches his Dad bludgeon his mother with his fists or a handy frying pan. Siblings huddle in their beds as the yelling and screaming keeps them awake long past their bedtime. Kids are ripped out of their beds in the middle of the night to flee the outrageous violence of a drunken father or a mother out of control. These occurrences are all too common.

Some kids never see the violence, but the tension around the supper table is palpable, because for the fifth or sixth night Mommy and Daddy aren't talking to each other. Children are hyper-sensitive to the emotional atmosphere around them, and find this tension destructive to their sense of security. Children of alcoholics who see Daddy being physically or emotionally abusive to mother while in his drunken state, build up fears and resentments toward the abusive parent. Seldom does separation or divorce come as a surprise to the children because their underlying anxiety, their fear of a divorce occurring between their parents is ever present.

Every child wants their parents to be in love with each other. A child's sense of security comes from the awareness that Mom and Dad are solid in their relationship. They watch for cooperation between them, for tender touch, for sharing of responsibilities and for signs that their parents care tenderly for each other.

Children learn from what they experience in their home and transfer what they learned there to the home they will establish later in life. In most cases, our ability as adults to demonstrate care, concern, cooperation and loving acts to our partner, was taught to us in our childhood home. Our ability to remain faithful to marriage vows and to "buckle down" to make a marriage work was instilled in us by watching our parents in their daily lives while we were growing up. Conversely, we can also learn, through a parent's choice of multiple partners, to give up on relationships when things don't go our way,

Childhood Abuse: Actual or Perceived: The words *mistreatment*, *violence, cruelty, neglect,* and *exploitation* are synonyms for the word *abuse*. More prevalent than we want to believe or acknowledge is the abuse received by little ones which is all too often perpetrated by a parent or significant family member.

Rejection, emotional, sexual and physical abuse (the four main categories of abuse) are perpetrated upon helpless children every day and in every town. We are pre-programmed to receive warmth, affection, tenderness and love rather than violence. When we receive pain rather than pleasure, a glitch occurs in the software of the computer-like brain. "Systems error" is written across the screens of our minds, and the computer brain malfunctions.

Worth and value are damaged as devastatingly as was New Orleans in Hurricane Katrina. Abnormal connections are made between the brain's neurons, and life takes a detour toward the negative side. Thoughts and feelings become more familiar with pain than pleasure. The mind longs for pleasure and gravitates toward it, and so children and adults re-program themselves to find that pleasure regardless of who gets hurt in the process. Thus, we see extreme self-centeredness, social withdrawal or the aggressive behaviors of unhappy children.

ADD and ADHD are deficiencies or malfunctions in the brain, but we now know that poor treatment sabotages the brain's ability to function as it was designed. And the tendency of society is to make the child "the patient" and medicate him or her, while the parents and the disrupted relationships from which they come go "scott free." Dr. Daniel Amen, a child psychiatrist, has identified six types of ADD, and according to him, it is easy to misdiagnose and treat wrongly. For more extensive information, see www.amenclinic.org.

Excessive Nudity (Modesty Not Taught) or Fear of Physical Exposure: Many people erroneously believe that they can walk around the house totally naked in view of their children. They think that it will be good for the kids and will not negatively affect them in any way. They are definitely wrong! Children are little sponges, absorbing all the information around them, and out of what they take in, they draw conclusions and make decisions.

When children are exposed to the sexual organs of the parent of the opposite sex before their brains can comprehend the concept of sexuality (which occurs during puberty) an inordinate curiosity is awakened in them. This curiosity becomes a drive toward things of a sexual nature. Parents should not be bathing with their children. They should not be sleeping with them beyond the first two years of life. Taking a child into the bed should be only for breast feeding or a brief snuggle, with parents clothed.

In the first place, sleeping with parents becomes a habit hard to break in a child, and in the second, it awakens a curiosity about sexuality. Sexual behaviors between the parents and nudity are for the privacy of the parent's bedroom, when the children are either asleep, in their own rooms or not at home.

At the other extreme are the parents who make it obvious that they are hiding something from their children. In other words, attention should not be given to things of a sexual nature either by nudity or undue secrecy. Minimize the attention given to sexual matters until the child is mature enough to understand the concept and purpose of sexuality.

Child Expected to Behave Older Than Their Age: "When will you ever grow up?" parents scream at their children. "Act your age!" "At your age you should know better!" A three-year-old is assigned to care for a newborn. A nine year old is expected to have the total care of her new baby brother. An older child is expected to care for the younger kids while Mom watches the "soaps" or busies herself with other things.

When a child is given adult responsibilities and expected to carry them out perfectly, this child becomes a workaholic and a perfectionist. Are we saying that a child should not have any responsibilities? Not at all! What we are saying is that the chores given should be age-appropriate and allow plenty of time for the child to engage in creative play and enjoy friendships with their peers.

While it is hard for many to comprehend, it is true that a child's work is their play. It is during their hours of play that they learn cooperation, teamwork, how to be a good sport and how to imagine, build and create.

Nancy, an only child, was expected to entertain her parents' and grandparents' adult friends on command and to be quiet when in adult company when parents chose that. Remember the old adage, "Children are to be seen and not heard"? This was the case in Nancy's family. She was often restricted from relating to peers and this created a hardship for Nancy when it came to friendships. It became easier for her to relate to older folks, while internally longing for peer friendships, which are especially important in the teenage years.

Child Left Alone Too Much or Never Left Alone: It is in the presence of emotionally healthy parents that a child feels loved and secure. It is through the interaction of the child with his parents that he learns what is acceptable and appropriate and what is not. The sense of belonging is established in those first couple of years of life, and the ever-present parent who will hold, cuddle, talk, caress and feed the child gives the child a strong message of significance. Hopefully, the Christian father believes that he stands in place of God to his child, and that his presence teaches the constant presence and availability of the Heavenly Father. His characteristics are interpreted by the child as those of God. We do know that the father is a powerful presence to the child. His love and affection are vital to the child's emotional health.

According to Dr. Thomas Verny in his book Pre-Parenting, speaking of a boy who was neglected and humiliated by his primary caregivers, "Lack of critical experience prevented development of the part of his brain that would have allowed him to feel connected to other human beings."

Babies who have the misfortune to be sent to orphanages after birth, lay alone and unattended in cribs, in rooms full of other unattended orphans. There without bright colored mobiles and other objects, constant attention by loving caregivers and sounds and touch to stimulate them, these infants bond to no one and vegetate without hope for a future. Their brains end up being significantly smaller that the brains of children in a healthy home with external stimuli, according to Dr. Daniel Amen, a leading expert in the field of child psychiatry.

On the other hand, children whose parents hover over them guarding them 24/7 come to feel that their parents have little or no confidence in their ability to be competent in any venture. "They don't trust me – they think I can't do anything!" The overpowering, overly protective parent who dogs the steps of his or her child, steals from him the desire to try, to achieve on his own. Feeling that he can't do right for doing wrong, the child can easily give up or become totally dependent on his parents, while being very resentful of the enmeshment.

Child Told "You're to be Seen and Not Heard": Have you been there? In previous generations, this used to be a prevalent philosophy. The basis for it was that children are empty, dumb, have nothing to contribute, and just need to be silent. "You're just a kid; what do you know?" was a frequent comment or question. In today's society, children are much more vocal, but, unfortunately, what they say is often disrespectful because they feel disrespected.

Still, the majority of society acts as though children do not have feelings, emotions or opinions. We have come a long way from the family unit as it was fifty years ago, to a fractured and scattered family, who comes together only occasionally for a family meal or a quiet evening of interacting and sharing. Cell phones. IPods, Game Boys, computers and a myriad of other techno-trivia take the place of genuine heart to heart conversation. This is a great disservice to children! We are not suggesting that because yesteryear's families were frequently together more than families are today, that they were more connected emotionally. History tells us that they were not appreciably more connected than families are today. They were engaged in work to survive and many were emotionally walled off, yet there was some sense of connection in the shared work they did.

Today, in most families, both parents work outside the home. Latchkey kids or after-school program kids, are separated from their families for hours during workdays. After-school sports, jobs and other activities, make even the stay-at-home mother a taxi service for activities. Order-in pizzas have replaced the sit-down family dinners and evenings of interactive games have been replaced by electronic amusements.

The opportunities for family interaction, for sharing of thoughts and feelings, for asking important and life-altering questions are few and far between. The amazing thing is that it is from the questions children ask that they learn important life answers and lessons. They need to be able to share their thoughts and feelings with an older and wiser caregiver. It is from these interactions, this sharing, that children learn to speak kindly and respectfully and receive age-appropriate answers to their questions. It is also from an open communication with parents, where they are not judged, evaluated, or humiliated, but responded to kindly and respectfully. These are necessary components to healthy emotional bonds.

One or Both Parents Alcoholic/ Drug addicted/ Workaholic or Religion-a-holic: All of these are addictions. An addiction is: a compulsion, a dependence, an obsession, a need or a craving. An addiction will take charge of a life and become more important than anything or anyone. A parent who has an addiction, is more concerned about satisfying his or her addiction than attending to the child. Being zoned out prevents needed emotional closeness. The addiction is all-consuming, and the child takes second or third place.

Many children of these parents are forced into responsibility far beyond their years. The mother who lies on the sofa, sipping vodka, smoking and watching the soaps, is paying little or no attention to her child. House cleaning and laundry are neglected to say nothing of food preparation! Children whose parents are drug addicted are likewise notoriously neglected, ignored and, all too often, beaten.

The workaholic parent places their career before their child, so, to the child, work is more important, more loved than the child is. The parent who is addicted to religion and/or their church places their religion in a more prominent position than their children. The wishes and longings of the child are secondary to the demands of the church or the standards of their particular religion. The child's requirements for socialization, for peer association, for attention and understanding from the parent or the church, are not taken into consideration. Again, the child interprets that they are unimportant.

One Parent Puts Child First and Neglects the Spouse: Children get their sense of security from the love relationship observed between their parents. The God-given software does not allow for a child to comprehend that a father would bring gifts to and be very affectionate with his little girl, but simultaneously ignore and be unaffectionate with his wife. The same would be true for a mother who gives all of her loving attention to her son while neglecting her husband.

While the attention feels good to the child, the lack of attention or the ill-treatment of the other parent is extremely hurtful to the child. Kids want Mom and Dad to be together and love each other. From this safety, a child develops a sense of security.

In situations where birth parents are divorced and remarried, children languish over their unsuccessful wishes and attempts to re-connect their parents. That wish lasts a very long time well into the late teens and beyond into adulthood.

Add to this that parents are always the models for their children, so when the children mature, marry and have children of their own, their inclination is to behave in the same manner with their spouses and offspring.

One Parent Does All the Discipline: So who was the tyrant in your family? Was your mother the one with the heavy hand, or was it your father?

In most households, either mother or father takes the lead or the responsibility when it comes to discipline. Often parents do not agree about just how heavy the hand should be, but the more dominant of the two will often be the one who wins that argument, and therefore the one responsible for the bulk of the discipline.

In Ron's childhood home, one of the children was singled out as the scapegoat. He took the punishment, the rod of correction, for all the kids. In that household, Daddy was the one with the rod of correction in his hand and mother gave him the excuses to beat the son. In Nancy's household, her mother would warn and then delay carrying out "the spanking" until Daddy came home. "You wait until your father comes home," was a frequently used threat, which was always carried out later by her father.

While one parent takes the label "bad guy" the other looks like a softer, gentler non-disciplinarian. Actually, each person has three sides to their personality. There's the victim, the rescuer and the perpetrator. When Dad is considered the perpetrator because he is the one doing the spanking, the child is the victim and that leaves the mother to be the rescuer – she will soften the blow or do the comforting following the spanking.

In a family situation, this is not good, because the parents are not in agreement. This disagreement creates insecurity in the child and also the opportunity for the child to play a divide and conquer game between parents. "I will get Mom on my side and thus be protected from Dad's punishments."

Child Feels Overly Responsible: In families of any size, children are frequently given responsibilities far beyond what they should be allotted. It used to be, in the days when parents had many children, that the eldest siblings were given the job of "watching out for" or tending the younger. Depending on the age of the eldest, these chores were often beyond their capabilities. All too frequently, they missed out on childhood themselves and adopted the work of adults. In the same families, the youngest children were "foot loose and fancy free" while the older ones became surrogate parents to younger siblings.

Comparing the burdens of the eldest and the younger children, the responsible ones often felt "put upon" and used rather than appreciated and doted upon like the youngest were. This is a form of rejection! Seldom were the labors of the older children appreciated and affirmed.

Another form of placing too much responsibility upon children is parents sharing with them the details or feelings about their marital relationship. Even without the sharing, children are sensitive enough to feel when the parents' relationship is not healthy, but when details are shared with them they have the added burden of trying to fix their parents' marriage. These attempts inevitably fail, and the child then takes the blame for the failure. In addition, the child receives the message that he or she is unable to help a spouse later in life, because of the early failure to fix a parent. The shadow haunts and sets the stage for failure.

Child Feels Smothered By One or Both Parents: Sometimes parents, out of their own emotional weakness or emptiness, overload their children (or one of them) with affection and overprotection. While affection is appropriate and acceptable in young children, there is an invisible line that parents can easily cross, which makes a child feel smothered.

As children approach puberty, they seek to move away from their parents to relationships with their peers. This doesn't mean that they cease loving their parents (even though it may feel so to Mom and Dad), but it does mean that peers become more important to teens than parents. If a mother should embarrass her son by being openly demonstrative with him when his friends are around, this is horrifying to the boy. The same is true with fathers and daughters or even parents of the same sex as the child. Somehow, it's "just not cool" to be that expressive with teens, especially in the presence of friends. In some families, parents place a child of the opposite sex in a surrogate spouse role. Here they share with the child information that is not shared with the marital partner. This burden, this weight of information is far too great for a child, and is very inappropriate on the part of the parent.

It may be difficult to see how public affection or clandestine conversations could make a child feel rejected, but when a child's wishes are ignored by his parent or when a child is expected to play a role that is inappropriate to his or her age and position, the child feels rejected because he is not allowed to be a child, but forced into an adult role.

Sibling Comparison: "What is the matter with you? Why can't you get good grades like your brother did?" "I wish you had a figure like your sister!" "Your sister is the pretty one," or, your brother is the smart one." These hurtful words and others like them are said daily in many homes around the world. How hurtful it is to be compared with someone else. "Why can't you play the piano like Zelda?", Nancy's father would ask. Nancy used to think, "I'm never going to be good enough to be equal with her. I'm just second class."

A young man by the name of Kip Kinkle, was regularly compared to his older sister, who was brilliant academically and a great athlete! Kip just couldn't "get" the math problems or succeed with the spelling words, and had "two left feet" when it came to athletics.

Kip killed his parents and then went to school and killed teachers and fellow students. Are we saying that this was the only reason that Kip murdered? No. However, it was a major contributing factor to the rage that built inside him, that caused him to commit the crimes.

We are all created equal. Some are given one gift and someone else receives a different ability. Each of us wants to be known and appreciated for who we were created to be, rather than to feel the sting of rejection that comes with being compared unfavorably with another.

Affection or Praise Based on Performance: Did you ever get the feeling that you had disappointed your parent? Perhaps the words were never audibly spoken, but you got the message loud and clear that your grades, your recital, or your behavior had been less than acceptable to your mother and/or father. Funny isn't it, that when you did great, you were seldom, if ever, praised, but when you goofed you really did hear about that?

Nancy recalls the horrifying moment when she got to the piano at her recital and could not think what she was to play. Paralyzed by fear, she slumped to her seat and could hear her piano-playing father sigh in disgust. He was embarrassed by her inability to perform. She recalls the silent ride home minus the promised ice cream cones, and then the lengthy "sermon" about how inept she was.

What was it like for you when your parents neglected to affirm or were fluent with the criticism? Did you feel loved and accepted?

Child Being Raised in Extreme Poverty or Wealth: Perhaps it is hard to comprehend that a child raised in a wealthy family would feel rejected like a child raised in poverty. What's the cause?

Living in either poverty or wealth makes one or both parents have their primary focus on money – not on the child. In a family that's well-off financially, Mom and Dad are focused on keeping and growing their bank account and investments, and in a poor family, the focus is on getting enough to be able to house, clothe and feed the family. Long hours are spent in retaining the fortune or on working hard enough to provide for everyone. In some poorer families the provider feels so much a failure that he doesn't even try to obtain a job or try to better himself. The example that the children get is of irresponsibility and resignation to failure when circumstances are difficult.

When the parents focus is on anything but their relationship and the training of their children, the children come secondary to the real focus. Unusually long hours away from home, distances the parents from the children, who in turn experience rejection.

Divorce of Parents: Abusive Parents: Children have a God-given need for both parents! In a situation where parents are not getting along in their marriage where there's adultery, fighting or abuse between them, children always fear that Mom and Dad will separate or divorce. The sad part is that when parents do divorce, the child takes 100% responsibility for the break-up! Because children are at the center of their world, they feel as though they caused the rift and should have been "good enough" to fix it.

When mother and father divorce, usually the custody of the children is given to one or the other with the other may or may not have visiting privileges. How difficult for the children to be shuttled back and forth between two houses and, in many cases, to become accustomed to a step-parent. Again, the child and his or her welfare is secondary to the selfish wants and desires of the adults.

Parents who abuse their children by outright rejection of them, by sexual abuse (known as incest), by emotional abuse (words said that do not uplift or edify or words unsaid – the silent treatment) or by physical abuse (any touch given without love, respect or dignity) reject their children. Each of the abuses produce feelings of rejection in the children.

Remarriage: Competition Between Child and Step-Parent: When a parent divorces and remarries or is widowed and remarries, the child is forced into a situation of second place. At that point, the parents focus on each other and are concerned about being a success in their marriage. The child is required to build a relationship with the new step-parent, while in many such situations the child is still wishing and dreaming that his or her birth parents would reunite.

In some cases, the child seems to welcome a substitute parent into the situation where there was a loss, but the readjustment is often very difficult for the child. Who gets the most attention – the new marriage partner or the child? Usually it is the new spouse who wins out while the child competes for attention from the birth parent.

Inconsistent Discipline: Inconsistency is conflicting and contradictory. When it relates to the discipline of children, the child seldom is able to predict the outcome of a choice or behavior they make. "Will I get spanked or beaten or punished, or not?"

To "disciple" is to make a child a follower, a believer, a devotee of the parent. Unfortunately, this type of discipline is seldom taught to parents and experienced by children. What occurs instead is punishment. Punishment is a sentence, a penalty or retribution. The parent, all too often in anger, punishes a child to assuage his own frustration. Very infrequently, does the punishment fit the crime. Instead, parents yell, swat with any handy instrument or their hand, slap the face, clobber the head, or beat rather than spank.

Spanking should be a last resort. Rather than drive a child to obedience with threats and physical torture, the parent should gently lead by example and reason.

A child like Ron's brother George, who went to bed night after night with bleeding cuts or blisters from the beating he had just received, does not forget the treatment he received. Resentments burst into full blown rage, and someone always pays the price for the rejection of the value and worth of the child. In George's case, everyone paid – his mother, his siblings, his wife, his children and the people from whom he stole what he wanted.

Now that you have read this, how would you rate your acceptance by your parents, friends, relatives, teachers and others? Please know that even if you check off a large number in this list, you are fixable. All that is required is a teachable spirit, so keep reading on!

Note:

"If pain and stress are damaging to the newborn (and he has previously explained that in his book: Pre-Parenting) *there are two situations where the two factors crescendo so alarmingly as in the NICU. In an ideal world, the premature infants placed in these centers would still be in the womb. There, they would sense muted light and sound against the backdrop of their mother's heartbeat and the undulating tightening of her uterus, increasingly snug with the baby's growth. Instead, NICU preemies are bombarded with bright lights and the jarring sounds of electrical machines and alarms yet left essentially untouched by caring hands in clinical bassinets. I am convinced that many preemies would be better off lying with their mothers than being placed in the noisy, aseptic milieu of the NICU, where they are constantly prodded by needles and stuffed full of tubes."*

Verny, Thomas. Pre-Parenting. (94)

Chapter Six

The Origin of Feelings

The chart below should be read from right to left. Ask yourself, "Do I . . . .?" Look on the list on the following pages to fill in the empty column. This is an exercise in understanding how your childhood is affecting you today.

Source of our Feelings & Behaviors

Damages occurred during the first seven years.

Damage	Character Defects	Our Behaviors
General Criticism	Lack the right to feel good about self. Lack the right to take risks	Tend toward perfectionism, procrastination, and settling for 2nd best.
Sibling/Other Comparison	Don't feel valued for who you are	Tend to have unhealthy relationships, lean toward materialism, and/or have a highly competitive spirit
Emotionally unavailable parents	A disbelief in possibility of intimacy. Afraid to trust Insecure	Relationships superficial. Tendency to sabotage relationships.
Feelings Discounted	Distrust of self and others. Ignorance of others feelings & a self destruction of our own feelings.	Emotional flatness. Emotions are pretended. An underlying feeling of estrangement from others.
Abusive touch / Frequent Spanking	Disbelief in personal safety. Unsafe touch normal.	Abusiveness to others. Emotional withdrawal. Sexual frigidity.
No Touch	A disbelief in true intimacy; Feel uncomfortable touching or being touched.	Dependence in most relationships. Tend to have a fear of commitment.
Body Shame	Feel the need to look/be perfect. Difficulty accepting self. Feels cannot make mistakes.	Obsessive about appearance, Excessive fear of aging.
Repeated, shameful behavior on the part of parents	Distrust authority figures or whatever feels like authority. Don't feel that "I belong".	Grandiose ideas. Feeling of being damaged and different. Chronic distrust and sense of insecurity.
Expected to know, seldom given time or instruction to learn	Fear of trying new things. Fear punishment for mistakes. Cannot make mistakes	A haunting sense of inferiority. Tend towards perfectionism. Pretended ignorance. Anxieties
Conditional Acceptance	Feel: I must be perfect. No right to refuse. No right to be tired	Hyper-responsibility. Denial of personal pain. People-pleasing.

Chapter Seven

Dark Glasses

Those who have experienced rejection tend to see the world through dark glasses. Everything they view has a negative downside, rather than a rosy-tinted, joyous expectation of the future. The rejected predict that everyone they meet will reject them. They search for the familiar rejection everywhere, and if they cannot find it, they will assume it anyway. This is the shadow that follows and forces them into wearing darkened glasses. In combination, the shadow and the glasses create quite a confusing and troublesome experience for those who are related to or married to the rejected one. It is as if the rejected are always looking for words said or left unsaid, facial expressions or body language, and even reading words and meanings into conversations, which might add ammunition to the case that they continue to build – that they are rejected.

Especially at times when a rejected individual is overwhelmed by responsibilities, overworked or emotionally distressed, the drive to discover rejection and to "pin it on someone close to them" is accelerated. Remember the law of the mind: "With every period of exhaustion, there's a corresponding period of depression, which goes to our weakest point at that moment." So for those who have been rejected, their weakest point is feeling rejected. That feeling may produce anger, fear, sadness and feelings of worthlessness. The anger is usually dumped on the one the rejected has determined is the perpetrator of rejection or the one emotionally closest to the rejected.

"What was then is now." This is an extremely important phrase to memorize. Why? The reason that this phrase is so valuable to our healing is that it helps to remind us that our reactions today are usually the result of what happened back when we were children. It was our childhood years and experiences that created the shadow or the darkened glasses through which we view and respond to what we are experiencing today. One of the best things you can do is to make a list of those who you feel rejected you at some time in your childhood. Alongside the name of the person, write a sentence or two that describes the incident in which you felt as though you were the victim. Then when we come to the chapter about healing from rejection, you will have a ready list to begin your healing process.

Ron tells about being rejected by his family. His parents did not want any more children. They already had three and were finding it very difficult financially to feed, clothe and house them. So, when the pregnancy with Ron was discovered, his Mother coped by denying that she was pregnant. Ron's father, who was working several hundred miles away from home, came home infrequently, but was a very angry man who screamed, pounded the furniture and swore a great deal. The atmosphere surrounding Ron in the womb was a frightening one. Mom denied his existence, Dad made loud and angry noises, and the message came through to him that he was not a wanted child.

When Ron was born weighing 10½ pounds, the delivery was difficult, and his Mother suffered physical complications as well as a postpartum depression or psychosis, making her pretty much out-of-touch with reality. His Mom's physical problems caused her lengthy hospitalization because she was critically ill and "on death's door" according to Ron's older siblings. When she was finally released from the hospital, Dad took her with him several hundred miles away to where he was working, and left Ron's care to his nine year old sister and a 16 year old nanny who came in while his sister was in school.

With this history, Ron surely could interpret that he was a rejected child, and so he did! Beginning at about age four, Ron's mother was back home and physically well again, and Dad was home from his wartime duties as well. Ron observed his Mother conspiring with his father against George, a brother eight years Ron's senior. She would sit on the cellar steps egging Dad on to beat George harder and longer for offenses for which he had already been punished. George and Ron shared a bedroom, and when George would frequently come to bed bleeding or blistered, Ron would feel devastated for his brother and hatred for the mother who had betrayed him. To make matters more devastating, their oldest sister would come into their room and hit George on the head with her high-heeled shoe to stop his moaning and groaning and rocking in his bed. While George was getting an overload of negative attention, Ron was being ignored -- sent off to the movies to get rid of him. Ron can't recall restrictions and definitely cannot remember being hugged, held or considered important

Dad had a violent temper, and seemed to be annoyed by everything. Laughter, children talking or playing together, sneezing, coughing, normal life sounds bugged Dad, and would provoke from him numerous expletives directed at whoever was making the sounds. Renata, Ron's mother, spent considerable effort to keep her husband from such explosions by banishing the children. Frequently, Ron would be given a quarter and sent to the movies. Twenty-five cents would buy a double feature and the cartoons and newsreels in between them, and he'd have enough left over for a bag of popcorn. Soon, Ron got the message that he was to disappear.

Peachy, the eldest sister was already married and gone from home, and Phyllis (Ron's surrogate mother) was gone from home with school activities and time with her boyfriend. The two boys were the ones at home. George was still receiving the beatings regularly. Ron was mostly the ignored and invisible one. On Christmas morning, Ron paddled down the stairs in his PJ's to see a train running around on a track under the tree. "That train is for you, Butch!" his father called out. He was so thrilled! He laid under the tree for several hours, mesmerized by the sound and the sight of it, but by noon, the train was gone, and he never saw it again.

Years later, Ron asked his brother-in-law, Johnny about that train and he replied, "Your Dad was just looking for some excuse to take it back to the store, because he really couldn't afford it. So he blamed you for doing some little thing wrong, and as a punishment took the train away and back to the store, where he got his money back. You got blamed, but it was really your Dad's doings, and not yours. Actually, your Dad did that a lot – that's what he did with a bike on George's birthday, too."

One day, when Ron was about six years of age, he was sent to the movies. His mother had been gone for several days and as usual, he did not know where or why. When he came home from the movies, his parents were both at home and so was a new baby.

Mother had been gone to the hospital and had given birth to a little brother they named Bobby. Mother's behaviors observed toward his new baby brother were entirely different from what he had experienced. She held and hugged him, spoke sweetly to him, and gave him an abundant amount of affection. Again, Ron was the outcast, the invisible one, and Bobby became Mother's treasured one, So it was until her death many years later, even though a daughter was born two or three years after Bobby.

Communication was greatly lacking between the parents and children, except for the demeaning and screaming directed at them. When Ron's grandpa died, "Butch", as he had been nicknamed by his father, was sent to the movies and came home to a crowd of people in his home drinking coffee and eating German pastries. He assumed that a party was going on and made himself scarce, as he had been forced to do at times such as this in the past. He was never told by his parents or his siblings, that while he was at the movies, Grandpa's funeral and burial had occurred.

A similar experience occurred when his best little friend, Tommy, a seven-year-old like himself, died from hemophilia. A few days after the funeral, Ron went next door to get his friend to come out to play, and Tommy's mother burst into tears when he asked for Tommy. Finally, it was she who told Ron about Tommy's death. There would be no more hours of "little boy joy" in the tree house they had shared together.

Shortly after Tommy and Grandpa's deaths, Ron's parents decided to move the family to a different house, more in the country. Butch was sent off to the movies. When he came home, a large truck was parked in front of their house, and the last of the family's possessions were being put into it. When Ron questioned what was happening, he was informed that the family was moving elsewhere. This was a particularly devastating blow to him because he and Grandpa had planted a little garden in the yard, and the flowers were just beginning to peek through the soil. When in tears he pleaded not to leave his treasured garden, his dad laughed at his pain and told him that they weren't staying at the house "just for a few stupid flowers!" Ron was devastated! Do you suppose that the torture he experienced that day affected his attitude towards gardening in his adult years?

To this little boy precious people and important things kept disappearing. A little boy begins to draw conclusions from such experiences. *When I get close to people or objects, they somehow get taken away. I must be the problem.* Unfortunately, that is an erroneous conclusion but one that is easily drawn and then cemented in a child's mind to become a shadow that follows, preventing close or intimate relationships.

The family's move took them from crowded suburbia to the country. Eventually, the boy who had become quite familiar with being a loner met several other kids his own age. Perhaps because one of the boys was named Tommy, Ron drew closer to him than the others. There were some happy times of countryside exploration and the love of a Labrador retriever puppy he named "Blackie". There was even a cat he became close to there. But the status of the family's interaction with each other remained unchanged.

Saturdays, Mom spent the majority of the day in the kitchen. There she would fill a large washbasin with her special pastry dough, and create from it pastries of every imaginable description. Apricot, raspberry and poppy seed filled Danish pastries, Kuechen and donuts covered every flat surface. The fragrance of her creations caused a little boy – or anyone else – to drool in anticipation of what was to come.

Toward evening, the neighbors began to arrive and the fragrance of freshly brewed coffee was added to the aroma of abundant pastries. The children were not allowed to touch the pastries. Mother would grab "Butch" by his hair when the first neighbor knocked, and he would be dragged to his bedroom and shut in with the door locked from the outside. There he was to remain for the rest of the night. A boy's curiosity caused him to press his ear against his door, listening for what was happening on the other side. The laughter he heard led to the conclusion in his mind, through the filter of rejection, that the friends were laughing at him because he'd been locked away. The pungent smells of baked goods and coffee created the yearning for participation in the group, but again, he had been isolated from friendship and participation in happy occasions. The sound of coffee being poured into cups around the dining room table, became a sound that when heard even in adulthood, sparked anger. Finally, as a defense against the building anger and resentment within him, he would fall into a troubled sleep, still locked in his room.

Ron doesn't remember how he acquired his very best friend – a puppy who was a cross between a black lab and a Springer Spaniel, but his sister thinks that he was given the puppy by a neighboring farmer. "Blackie" was his constant companion, his confidant, his best friend and together they roamed the Arkansas countryside. When the pup was several years old, Stanley, Ron's father, decided to finish the basement of their house and create a bar and a family room there, where he would entertain family and friends. One weekend, Johnny came to help with the construction process. Blackie was down in the basement because Ron was there helping too.

An extension cord had been laid across the room to run a piece of electrical equipment, and Blackie repeatedly tripped over the cord. Johnny warned that they should tape the cord to the floor, but Stanley resisted loudly. After tripping one too many times, Blackie grabbed that cord in his mouth and bit down. Johnny raced to the wall and removed the plug from the socket, but it was too late – the damage had been done. Blackie wasn't the same after that. "It ruined that dog's life," Johnny said years later. So how did the family cope with the change in Blackie, who no longer allowed anyone near him except Ron? They sent Ron to the movies, and when he came home, Blackie was gone. To this day, the fate of Blackie has not been discovered. Johnny and Phyllis think that he was taken to the humane society to be "put to sleep." There were to be no tears and no expressions of grief at the loss.

There at his country home on Waukesha Road, Ron's friend Tommy contracted polio, and was hospitalized in an iron lung for a while before his death. Ron was not taken to see his friend or allowed to attend his funeral. For Ron, people just came and went, and the experience of intimate connection, of emotional attachment, was discouraged and faded into nonexistence.

A loss occurred again when the family cat had a dozen kittens. Off to the movies he was sent again and when Ron returned the cat and her twelve kittens had been drowned. What sort of message does a child get from repeated episodes like these? *People and relationships of all kinds are disposable, and one is not to grieve over the loss – grieving is for the weak. Actually, it is better to not allow yourself emotional connection with an animal or human, and then you won't have to grieve at their loss.*

Renata became very ill. Over a few weeks, she broke out in a violent rash all over her body from great emotional stress. There was something about her life experiences that finally was taking its toll on her. Endeavoring to keep Stanley from violent episodes and all the while assuming that he was involved with other women, was too much of a weight upon her. There had to be an escape. There had to be some relief from the craziness and the fact that George had become a criminal, and Butch was saying that he wanted to be just like George. So the next move was planned.

Arkansas was quite a distance from the stress of home, so Stanley and Renata's brother, decided to buy a little motel together in Arkansas. Again the family packed up and moved off to a distant state "for Renata's health." At this point, Butch was in seventh grade, and had already been in some minor scrapes with the law like stealing a few apples from the neighbor lady's orchard – dropped apples at that! He had been to her door and asked her if he could pick up some of the drops for his Mom to make a pie. She refused and warned that if he stole them she would send the police after him – and so she did. But when the police came she said as she stood in Renata's kitchen, "If only he had asked I would gladly have let him have the drops." What a lie, and what a message to the child. *Tell the truth and you get punished, but others can get away with lying and you will pay the price for their lies.* Here was another experience of woman betraying him as his mother had done to George. So the second message he received was *you cannot trust a woman. They will betray you every time.* That message was to become a life commandment, part of the daunting shadow that set him up for repeated difficulties with women in his life. And you can be sure that his trust in his mother was gone by this point.

For a while, living in Arkansas seemed to be a happier existence than living up north. Even though the sale of the motel fell through, Stanley was able to find sheet metal work and then wound up buying the business. Ron got a paper route, started taking babysitting jobs and hung around with a few “sick” guys, as he terms them. They were into sexual experimentation, and, for the third time in his short life, he was molested: this time by those who were supposed to be his friends. Escalating rage within him began to seep out into his behaviors.

One more experience occurred which finally tipped the scales in Ron’s behaviors. His birthday was coming up, and since he had never been given a birthday party in his thirteen years, he decided to plan his own party. He purchased a cake and some drinks with his paper route money, and invited several friends to his house for the party. Unfortunately for him, his Dad came home as they were seated around the table eating birthday cake. Dad threw a fit. In a screaming rage, he demanded that the kids go home, and, to be sure, they scattered. After they left, he forced Ron to return the yet unopened gifts they had brought to each of them. Obscenities punctuated his rage and again Ron was reduced to worthlessness as, totally embarrassed, he walked from door to door to return the gifts. In his mind was the thought that had repeatedly crossed his mind in the past, but this time was set in cement and destined to become even more than a shadow; it would be a template that would orchestrate future behaviors – *he was worthless!* He determined that he would "take" what he wanted instead of waiting to receive. Receiving meant it would be taken away. After all, hadn't that been the case with the train, with George's bike, with Blackie and with his cat and her kittens and with the birthday presents? His rationale was, *If I don't receive it from someone else, it can't be taken away. If I get it on my own, no one can take it away. Therefore, I will either take or buy what I want!"* And thus began his next few years of crime.

By the time Ron was just coming into his teen years, when children normally drift away from the close bond and association they have with parents to a close bond with their peers, Ron was gone. As far as he was concerned, there had been no close association with his parents at all. The closeness with Phyllis in his character forming years, which he doesn't even remember, was gone because she too had deserted him when he was seven to marry Johnny. Ron was a loner having been forsaken by even his friends in death. His escapades of stealing were totally on his own – not in a gang which is typical of the teen years. He had come to the conclusion that the way to live life was alone, hard-heartedly taking what you want.

Reviewing your years up to age thirteen, with whom were you emotionally connected or bonded? Who were your best friends in childhood? Do they remain "best friends" still today? Do you recall experiences of rejection like Ron's? Have you experienced numerous losses? Review those and compare your beginnings to his. Were yours similar or different?

In the next chapter, we will look at rejection from another angle, and if you didn't find similarities to Ron's experience, you may find yourself in this next chapter.

What messages do you suppose Ron got about women from his earliest experiences? Later, as he began to grow and his father had completed his wartime duties and moved back home, how much trust could he possibly have in the consistency, the commitment and the loyalty of women as a whole? Don't you think that he would be somewhat fearful of the emotional and physical devastation that a woman could cause in his life, to say nothing of their willingness to stay with him?

Well, to be sure, Ron knows the trauma of rejection and the negative, thundercloud thoughts that result from feeling unloved and unwanted. The fear of being abandoned did haunt him for several years in our marriage, but the process of recovery has made a transformation in his experience! Do the thoughts come up after years of recovery and a stable marriage? Yes, especially when he is exhausted, BUT the difference now is that the thoughts do not control his reactions and behaviors. He has learned to say "what was then is now." He asks himself, "what exactly happened then that is accelerating this current experience into more than what it is?" He will recall an experience, write about it or share it verbally with someone else, and that destroys the negative charge in the emotion that would have controlled his behavior. His shadow continues to disappear.

Ron's story is more blatant -- more obvious -- than some others. Let's take a look at Nancy's history – her experiences of rejection.

Chapter Eight

It Keeps Coming Up!

Rejection has more than one face. It is like a gemstone with multiple facets. Whether overt or covert, it destroys the worth and value of the one who experiences it, because its shadow always follows. Perhaps the more subtle and insidious the rejection the harder it is to define and understand, therefore leaving its victim questioning if they are really experiencing rejection.

Nancy was the first child of a young couple who dearly loved each other, and although married, they were separated by the husband's call to duty in the armed services just before the start of World War II. When Nancy was seventeen months of age, her father was shipped off to Europe and the front lines of a war now in full force. Her exposure to her father had been minimal at best, because he was stationed miles from home, so her comprehension of her father's position in her life was nonexistent. It was only through the frequent calling of her attention to her father's picture on the mantel and the labeling of the person in the photo as "Daddy" that Nancy knew that this man was Daddy. The truth is that her little girl mind thought that every man in an army uniform was Daddy. The title meant nothing to her.

When the war was over and Jim returned to the United States, a great deal had taken place in the little family to whom he returned. His wife Ena had been pregnant when Jim was shipped overseas, and her pregnancy had ended with the birth of their son,

James Robert. Ena had experienced a difficult pregnancy, one tainted with the fear of her husband's emminent death in a German foxhole. One month prior to her due date, the placenta began to tear from her uterine wall, and her son was born a month early weighing 4 lbs. 10 oz. He was a healthy child who did well, but Ena was frail and had infectious hepatitis. Because of her illness and her son's prematurity, the doctor ordered that he be fed by tube, so that Ena could rest. At one of those feedings the tube was inserted into his lungs rather than his stomach, and his lungs were filled with formula, causing his death.

There were months of mourning in Nancy's little family comprised of her mother and the grandparents with whom she lived. Mother was sent home shortly after her son's death, but remained quite ill for nearly a year. The family's attention shifted from Nancy to the loss of little Jimmy and Ena's care, as would be expected under the circumstances. A sense of sadness and loss pervaded their home and attitudes.

Finally, the war ended and Jim returned home in full dress uniform. Ena was transformed by his presence, since for several years she had feared she would never see him again. Within two days, he had found an apartment and moved Ena and Nancy to that apartment away from the grandparents who had a significant part in her upbringing. Nancy was four years old at the time of that move.

Finally, for the first time since their wedding, Jim and Ena were "setting up housekeeping" and living together in their little apartment. In order to afford a place of their own, Ena went back to work as a nurse part time in the evenings, and Jim worked days. This was definitely a new experience for both Nancy and her father. He had really never known his little girl and she did not know him. To her, he was a newcomer. He brought with him from the front lines his Master Sergeant tactics of control. Nancy had been treated tenderly before his return, but now she was to march to the beat of a different drummer.

"Poode", as he called her, could do nothing right. He demanded that she eat **all** the food she was served, regardless of the fact that something would gag her and cause her to vomit. That he himself had a finicky appetite bore no weight; she would do as he said, not as he did. Either he laughed at her blunders or tormented her because of them. He was an exceptional pianist and wanted her to follow in his path, but his determination pushed her farther away from his desired goal and frequently shoved off of the piano bench. He was careful to not treat her harshly when Ena was around, and it wasn't until Nancy was thirteen years of age that Ena saw for the first time how Jim behaved and felt toward her. It happened with a reactionary slap across Nancy's face, because she rolled her eyes in in disgust following a comment that Jim had made. In later years, Ena admitted that she was devastated when that slap occurred. Through her teenage years, Nancy was depressed, overweight, traumatized with sexual abuse by two old neighborhood men and had her activities greatly controlled by her family. This continued until high school graduation.

College, nurse's training and graduate school passed, with Nancy living away from home. Then there was her wedding and a subsequent move out of state. Years later, in Jim's sixty-sixth year, he told his only child, that she was a great disappointment to him, and one half hour after that comment he was dead in her arms. Those were his last words to her.

You might say that Nancy's rejection wasn't so subtle, but there was a complication. The difficulty was that rejection was mixed with affection from her father and, most of the time, she experienced love and acceptance from her mother. Actually, Jim was on a very tall pedestal in Nancy's eyes, because he was talented, intelligent and so loved and admired by others including her mother. She had been taught that her father was a very special man who should be admired under all conditions. Considering all of this, Nancy was confused!

It took until the time of her father's death for Nancy to be able to take a realistic look at her relationship with her father and analyze it for the truth of its emotional pain. Once reality hit her, Nancy wallowed in pity and in resentment toward the man she'd both admired and resented, but that was short-lived. The shadow of old and new pain would haunt her and impact her relationship with her husband until she began a healing process. Recovery will move us on to understanding of others and once we have emptied our angst, there is room for us to receive forgiveness for the offender.

Answers from family members both in the United States and in England, where her father was born and lived until he was eight years old, gave her an understanding of his beginnings and the major rejection he had received from his parents, particularly his mother. There was not a day in Jim's life when he felt accepted by his mother. Until her death, he visited her every day after work hoping for acceptance. Even after a stoke left her in an aphasic state, she would shake her finger at him and, in a disgusted tone, would grunt, "Da-da-da-da-da!" Anyone listening clearly knew her negative attitude toward her son.

Once her father's beginnings and experiences of rejection were understood, Nancy moved toward looking at *her* rejection of her father. What part did she play in the relationship? What had she contributed to the emotionally disconnected relationship? As she began the process of looking back, she realized that she had only entered the relationship when her father returned from the war, and immediately had resented his intrusion into her comfortable little life. Not only had he arrived on the scene ready and determined to take charge of his little family, but he had also removed her from her safe place and the adoration of her grandparents. He had come into the relationship like a lion, and she took exception to his power and dominance. She was not allowed to display her anger, so she play-acted love and acceptance. Occasionally she enjoyed fun experiences with him, but the majority of their relationship was on a serious level with him as the domineering presence and her as the subservient and obedient child. She had pushed him away in her mind, and, on some level, he as the rejected child, knew it.

Like it or not, we carry the scars of our parents', grandparents' and great grandparents' behaviors and attitudes. "What? Are they in our shadow too?" you ask. The only way to change this is to choose to confront reality, investigate the system that set up the person who harmed us, and come to an understanding of the pain of the perpetrator. Mind you, this is not letting the perpetrator "off-the-hook" nor is it denying the magnitude of your hurt. Rather, it is coming to comprehend the reason for the behavior. *A reason is the set-up. An excuse is a cover-up.*

Be assured, that it is never wise to excuse the behavior of someone who preys upon us. Not only do we carry the blemish of our predecessors, but we also pass theirs and ours on to our children. They will bear what we have as well as what we added to the mix. Our responsibility is to say, as did President Truman, "The buck stops here!" "Enough of the craziness - It's time to solve this mess and move ahead toward emotional healing."

Perhaps the most devastating thing about rejection is that it keeps coming up! Once rejected, especially in the early years when character is being formed (conception through the seventh year of life) individuals are sensitized to rejection. A victim can always sense rejection by the slights, the looks, the comments and the body language of others. The filter through which they see life is colored by rejection, and their shadow dictates that they identify it..

Individuals who do not feel accepted often display their pain in attitudes designed for self-protection, yet those attitudes are usually the very thing that will cause them to be rejected again and again.

Perhaps it would be wise, if you are a victim of rejection, to begin to ask yourself what part you play in the rejection that you currently may experience. You just might discover that by changing your attitude, you can change your life.

Chapter Nine

You Can Choose Acceptance!

Do you find yourself at an intersection? You can go right or left. Which way will you choose? Will you opt for the familiar, albeit problematic direction? Or will you dare to step out onto a road not yet traveled?

Let's begin at the beginning. You have already come to understand that as you gain knowledge, you gain power. So here's a little more that will help you to identify just where you are on the journey to wholeness to recovery from your feelings of rejection..

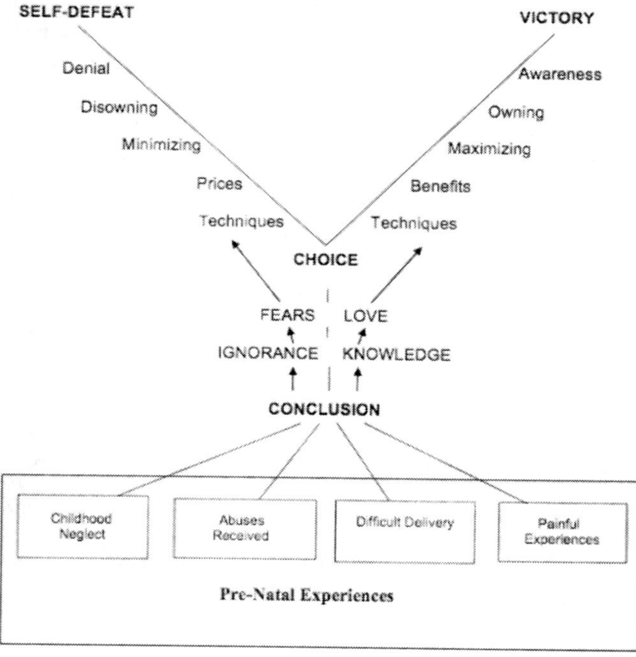

Conclusion – Early on in life, from the in-womb experience on through the first couple of years, each child draws a conclusion, a decision about his or her worth and value. This decision is based on all of the interactions experienced with Mother, Father, Grandparents and/or others prominent in the child's life. If a child is totally cared for, loved and accepted completely, he or she will conclude that he has worth and value in the eyes of his parents or primary caregivers. If a child is ignored, abandoned, disregarded, not adequately cared for or responded to when a need is expressed, the child concludes that he has little or no worth or value. Unfortunately, the latter is more the case than the former. Here enters also, the eventual belief system, the shadow of a teen or adult, that there is a God who cares or there is not. This is due to the fact that a child places parents in the place of God in those early years, and then transfers his conclusions about his parents to his spirituality and view of a Higher Being.

Ignorance – Because the conclusion is drawn when a child is still young, he is without information to make a rational choice. He only knows the path that his conclusion sets him on, so he moves forward on the road to self-defeat, an alarming choice. Developing self-protective techniques will not help long term, but will offer false hope of being safe and secure at first. The reason is that the techniques created are usually, in and of themselves, defeating of health, relationship success, job security etc. In most cases, the choices of techniques are made from the platform of fear.

Fears – To be sure, a child who faces the future alone, without the love and guidance of caring parents, has cause for worry. Out of the conclusion that one has little or no worth and value, comes a fear of being isolated, ignored. That fear will produce behaviors that either demand attention (usually negative behaviors) or the child will choose to meet his own needs as best he can, isolating himself or withdrawing from others. Fear is the foundation of anger, yet anger displayed causes more isolation. Fear causes people to focus on self-survival, and, since the brain is designed to see to it that the human survives, there's no choice but to protect oneself.

Choice – A life based on fear is destined to follow the road to self-defeat. Unhealthy fears, irrational fears, always predicting a negative outcome lead the individual down a slippery slope until he finally experiences the outcome he has been predicting. And here begins the development of techniques that guarantee him ending in self defeat.

Techniques – "I must survive so I will . . .

- build a wall of protection around myself so no one can harm me."
- numb my discomfort with tobacco, alcohol or drugs."
- fill my emptiness with food."
- connect with others by having lots of sexual experiences."
- use anger, sarcasm, criticism and an air of superiority to keep others distant."
- work continuously to prove my worth and value."
- etc., etc.

Prices – For every survival technique we establish we will pay a price. A wall of protection will cost us intimate relationships and create loneliness. Numbing our pain with substances costs us money, brain power, jobs and relationships. Filling up emptiness with food costs us our health and our appearance. Multiple sexual encounters with various partners cost us our reputation, our health and emotional pain. Anger, sarcasm, a critical spirit and an air of superiority costs us healthy and satisfying relationships. Continual work costs us our health, our attitude and healthy relationships. On and on it goes, experiencing loss after loss until very little of value is left in life.

Minimizing – "Oh, the price I have to pay isn't so bad! I'm better off with people distant from me; at least I won't get hurt all the time." And "That was a lousy job anyway and the boss wasn't fair, so I'll look elsewhere." "Bet I have more sex than most married people. I'm the lucky one!" And on and on – you get the picture. There are excuses and cover-ups for the cost of using dysfunctional techniques to keep the self safe. What really is happening is that the one who minimizes is constantly placing himself at risk.

Disowning – Picture the ostrich (or the human) with his or her head in the sand, and that's exactly what you have with an individual far enough down the road to self-destruction that he has arrived at this spot. "I don't have a problem. You're the one with the problem." "I am not losing my friends!" This is a process of pulling away from reality and further from those who they think can hurt them. In their minds, they have set others up to be "the problem."

Denial – This is a dangerous place to be! Here, people live totally out of touch with reality and in their own unreal world, dictated to them by their shadow. To the person in denial, everyone seems to be at odds with him. Being "always right" leads him to deny that there is anything wrong with him. "I'm alright, it's just the world that's all wrong" is his or her attitude. "I'm not a workaholic and I do not rage at others – unless they deserve it." These individuals end up being grumpy old men and "witchy" old women who lack friends, because no one wants to be around them! What a way to end life!

Twice divorced, a senior citizen we know lives alone and isolated. Each month, she receives checks from Social Security and a pension, yet she hoards her money, won't give the driver of the senior bus a tip, has made everyone think she is financially destitute, refuses to take care of her appearance, and is nasty to everyone she meets! She has a daughter and son-in-law who are willing to buy a little house for her, pack her up and move her to where they live, supplying her with a sunnier outlook and a little place to do the gardening she loves. And will she allow that? NO! She would rather be a hermit and miserable than to have happiness in her "golden" years. Do you suppose that she considers that this pathetic lifestyle is what she's worth? Do you think that her shadow has overtaken her?

So, this is where the road to self-defeat leads. Do you find yourself here or anywhere on the road? Be careful! Don't deny too quickly. Remember, the tendency of those on the road to self-defeat is to say that they are not on that road. Remember, too, that rejected people expect rejection – they think they are worth that too!

"How can I get off this highway," you ask. There's only one way. Turn around and go straight back to your conclusions. It was there in your conclusions that you first believed the lie that your worth and value is minimal. That's what needs to be changed. So you must examine the details of how you came to believe that you are worth very little and would have to survive on your own with no one else to help you – the contents of your shadow. Once you undo the lie and give it back to those who gave it to you, you can head for the road to victory. Let's take a look at it!

You are back at the conclusions, way down at the bottom of the Y. Let's say that you have examined your beginnings and you know for sure how you came to believe the lie by acknowledging the early experiences in the foundation of your conclusion. You have asked the questions that pertain to your time in the womb and you have some answers. Let's also say that you have given the lie back to the one(s) who gave it to you.

You let go of ignorance and begin to **Get knowledge**, (Remember? Knowledge is power) so now you have a driving force behind you to urge you onward.

Fear is replaced by hope and love. The opposite of fear is love, and when love becomes the foundation of your beliefs, you cannot fail! Love produces hope for the future, and so now with a positive outlook, you move ahead.

We come now to that fork in the road – **Choice.** When you were operating out of fears, there really was no choice for you – it is as if you were doomed to take the left fork to self-defeat. But now with added knowledge, you can make an intelligent decision – you can take the right road! You can decide to dump your shadow!

Why would you choose to develop techniques for self-protection (the next step toward self-defeat) when you can reap the benefits of being free from addictions (those techniques that tear you down)? You can begin to form **healthy techniques**.

Instead of paying a price in money, health or relationships you can **Benefit** from the new techniques you have developed. What a pleasant change!

Now, instead of minimizing your techniques you can **maximize** your benefits. How do you do that? When the changes start occurring within you, you will know and so will others around you. You cannot keep quiet about the changes in your life. Each step is lighter, burdens are cast off and you are enjoying relationships and friendships perhaps for the first time in your life!

You can **own** your own life now instead of being controlled by fears of others, of rejection and loss, and of the future. You are a person in victory. Instead of repeating, "I am an alcoholic or a sex-a-holic, you can lay claim to recovery – to victory. And you will win!

You now become **aware** of everyone around you. Rather than being focused on your little world of one, and all of its neediness, you become interested in and concerned about others. You become sensitive to the pain and dysfunction that you see in others and anxious to do something -- anything -- to help them. You begin to observe and question the actions of others, and wonder why you waited so long to begin your own healing.

Your life is changed, new, transformed, and count on it, you will NEVER turn back to the road to self-defeat again! What would be the point of that?

But wait a minute. You don't have the tools to recover from the pain of rejection yet, do you? By now, you are simply aware that you want to get on the right road, correct? Well, hold on, because recovery is on its way. Just turn the page!

Chapter Ten

"Out of the Shadow!"

Let's remind you that your God-given desire to belong has been sabotaged if you are a victim of rejection. Rejection pushes you away from an intimate relationship with the person who rejects you, and if that's your mother or father the blow is all the more devastating. And rejections experienced throughout life always bring up the initial rejection by parent(s) and add emphasis to what you are currently experiencing.

1. <u>Remember your beginnings.</u>

Recalling the past can be a blessing or a curse! But a great Christian author once said, "The greatest thing we have to fear is that we forget the way the Lord has led us in the past." George Santayana's famous quote reads,

"Those who forget the past are doomed to repeat it."

If you cannot recall your early childhood, then do a bit of Sherlock Holmes' work – start investigating. You can carefully inquire from family members who were present at the time of your birth, infancy and early childhood. Ask simple questions first, so as to not alarm them – especially if there is some painful history that they are attempting to hide or excuse away. You are simply endeavoring to get this information so that you can understand yourself better. Ask for pictures they might have, and if they don't want to part with them, ask permission to scan them or reproduce them so that you can own copies.

Does this sound frightening to you? Look at it this way: Ignorance is not always bliss but knowledge always gives us power! Determine that what might be temporary emotional pain from what you may discover, will give you long-term relief and personal understanding. Determine to face the pain and walk through it. Remember that you can walk through the valley of the shadow of death and God has promised to be with you. There's no greater protection and comfort that this!

Another idea that is helpful and fun is to start a scrapbook of pictures and short stories or quotes from older family members. If you don't have their picture, take one if they are still living or ask a relative to copy a picture he or she might have, and place in the scrapbook alongside their quote. This is a less threatening exercise than just "digging for dirt", and might be more easily accepted than just a question and answer session.

DO THIS: **Make a list of all the people who you feel have rejected you beginning with the first people in your life – your parents. Even if you were given out for adoption at birth, you should include your birth parents. Children who are given to adoptive parents, given to foster care or to an orphanage, are rejected children. Once the list is written, rewrite it and put it in chronological order. This list will come in handy shortly as you begin the active work of undoing the negative emotional charge in your memories of rejection.**

2. Write your story - or record it verbally into a tape recorder.

Your childhood was the set-up and forms the shadow that has been following you. Telling yourself the truth and then writing it and seeing it in writing begins to shed light into the shadow's darkness.

"The hand will write what the mouth cannot speak"

Perhaps writing frightens you because it was not one of your strongest subjects in school. There's something that you need to remember here, however - you aren't writing a book or a term paper and this project will not be receiving a grade. This is a process designed only with you in mind. It is about emptying all of the sadness, guilt, anger, and resentments that are stored along with the sight, sound, taste, touch and smell of your memories. It is about destroying the shadow so that you can enjoy the light of acceptance.

What you need to understand, is that we do not really forget. And that everything we have ever experienced, even the in-womb happenings are present in the memory bank, along with their accompanying senses and emotions. That's a whole lot of stored info, isn't it? It is the emotions attached to the memories that drive our thinking patterns, feeling states and behaviors.

The purpose of this exercise is to empty the negative emotions from the memories. Talk them out on paper or into a tape recorder. You certainly can talk them out with a therapist, and for some that is very helpful. Therapy may take abundant time and financial resources, so a thick notebook and a pen or pencil, make an inexpensive but highly effective processing tools.

DO THIS: **Write specifically about your experiences of being rejected. Use your list and start writing at the top of the list about the rejection from each individual. In your writing, include specific examples of how the person rejected you. Write about where you were, who was involved or present, your age at the time, the feelings you recall that took place in your body and your response at the time the rejection occurred. Where did you go, what did you say or do? And then, attached to each experience, discuss how what happened then has affected you down through the years to the present time.**

3. <u>Retrace the pain</u> – the feelings, the sadness, the anger, the helplessness. **Allow yourself to feel the feelings.**

They probably won't feel very good, but they are yours, and they've been running around in your mind, wounding your heart and destroying your health for a long time. So go ahead, cry, rage, grieve or whatever is appropriate, and then describe it in words or pictures on paper, or into a tape recorder. Confession is good for the soul, and liberating to the mind and heart! If these negative feelings are inside you, unexpressed and following you in your shadow, they will sabotage your physical and mental health.

Dr. Hans Eysneck of the University of London, calling upon his years of research, states that unresolved emotional issues are six times more predictive of coronary heart disease, high blood pressure, diabetes and cancer than is a poor diet or lack of exercise.

So feel the feelings, get some support from a family member, friend or counselor and begin your physical, emotional and mental healing! It's time to acknowledge feelings, quit denying their existence, and then let 'em go!

DO THIS: **As you are writing about the experiences of rejection, allow yourself to go back to those experiences in your mind's eye. See the scenes, and allow your body to recapture what it felt like then. Here you are breaking through the secrets that have been lurking in your shadow.**

Write about the sensations you are feeling now -- emptiness, pain in the gut, physical pain somewhere else in the body, hunger, nausea, coldness, or excessive heat. Write about these sensations as they appear. Here we are not speaking of thoughts or emotions. We are speaking of the rejection as it shows itself in your body. The amazing thing is that the cells of the body carry emotional pain, and you are in the process of recognizing just where your emotional pain hides in your body.

4. Recognize your current pain and the need for healing.

Pain has a purpose.

It clues us that something is wrong.
It sends us to the doctor for diagnosis.
It forces us into treatment to get rid of the problem.

Emotional pain has a purpose - the same as physical pain. Discover that ailment that is causing your symptoms, and share that information with someone else whom you trust. Speak aloud the words that need to be said, cry the tears, grit your teeth (but not too hard!)

A brisk walk or swim will help you to get out some of the anxiety that your body's cells are holding onto, causing you physical pain and disease. Then after the walk or swim, enjoy a nice warm bath or shower, some relaxing music and a cup of tea. Sit in your favorite chair and speak aloud words of thanksgiving that you have given yourself permission to heal and to share your history and pain with someone who is trustworthy and cares enough to listen.

ASK YOURSELF THESE QUESTIONS, AND ANSWER IN WRITING:

- **Do you find that you are often unable to eat, nauseated or perhaps you feel empty most of the time?.**
- **Have you noticed physical symptoms related to this, such as anorexia, bulimia or eating excessively so that you are overweight?**
- **Are your relationships in trouble? Do you have difficulty holding onto an intimate relationship with a spouse or loved one?**
- **Do you find yourself addicted to substances or behaviors that seem to make you feel better, at least for a little while?**
- **Do you see yourself as obsessive or compulsive, just having to do certain things in order to feel safe or comfortable?**
- **Do you work hard in order to prove your worth?**
- **Do you seek out multiple sexual partners trying to fill your emptiness with sexual connections?**

The sad thing is that these techniques we use are about survival, but we always end up paying quite a price for the technique we use. The individual who tries to fill emptiness with food, discovers that the food lasts for just a little while and then he needs to fill again, piling more and more calories into his swelling body. Soon the price paid is obesity and all of the complications that come with it such as diabetes, coronary heart disease, high blood pressure, cancer, joint degeneration, to say nothing of being ostracized from society due to appearance. The body demands nourishment when babies are new and growing, and when they don't get it, the longing and need for food is overwhelming! One of the main causes of obesity is the attempt of a needy individual to fill an emptiness that doesn't seem to get filled for more than a couple of hours at a time. Usually, the chosen food is high in fat and sugar and leads to major weight gain. An out-of-control body that's out-of-shape only asks for more rejection, stares, and snide comments.

The truth is that we tend to listen to the messages in our bodies more than the intellect or logic of our minds. The body demands touch and tenderness, and if we didn't receive it in infancy and childhood, we will demand it in teenage and adult years. Many young women turn to prostitution to fill a need, yet find that the "johns" love them and leave them, thus tagging on another rejection to what they already have.

The need for acceptance and approval is so great that women will starve themselves, or change body shapes by plastic surgery and invasive procedures. Some will do anything so long as they get the admiration they desire. Do you suppose that might be a function of never meeting up to a parent's excessive demands?

DO THIS: Which of the difficulties are you experiencing, and just how desperate are you to change the habits and get on the road to victory. Write about that.

In a book written by Carol Thuman entitled *Feelings Buried Alive Never Die,* Carol speaks specifically about body memories and the multiple diseases that we get by storing emotionally devastating memories in our bodies. She claims that most diseases are the result of unhealed emotions, and we agree! So do many physicians who claim that emotional stress is a major contributor to 90% of illnesses.

5. <u>Seek help from a good Christian Counselor or Pastor</u> and/or <u>get into a recovery group.</u>

There you'll be encouraged to do all that steps the course offers - you'll do the work of self-examination.

Sometimes, actually quite frequently, we need outside assistance in the process of recovery! We strongly suggest a small, supportive group, but not one where you go to simply and repeatedly rehearse your experiences and your pain. You will want to be in a place where you can be heard and where there will be a process that will move you from point A to point B and on through the whole recovery.

If you should need the assistance of a professional counselor however, we urge you to seek out a well-recommended one, and still to continue work through this book and/or in a small group for recovery. *Binding the Wounds* and *The Journey* are two we recommend, and are available at www.fixablelife.com

If you decide that you need one-on-one counseling sessions, please consider finding a counselor of the same sex as yourself. Usually this works out best for the therapist and for the client. If you are a female and you are choosing your male pastor, ask that his wife, your husband or a trusted friend be present in the session.

Rejection can be quite insidious and is often a conundrum not only to those who are experiencing it but also to counselors. Because it can be dumped on us in overt or covert ways, it is sometimes difficult to recognize, and, sometimes harder still to admit. Or as we said earlier, sometimes it is encased in abundant affection, and receiving that double message is so very confusing, especially to a child who cannot think in concepts or discern innuendos and insinuations. That is why victims often need someone to walk alongside them who will gently assist them in walking out from under the camouflage of double messages and innuendos and out of the shadow into the light of true understanding.

6. Get Knowledge.

Read Books – There is a wonderful list of Recommending Reading. Avail yourself of the opportunity to get more and more knowledge. It never hurts to read, apply the information to you, your history and your current thoughts, feelings and behaviors. The more that you understand yourself and what exactly has orchestrated who you are the better is the opportunity for change and improvement!

Recommended Reading for Rejection:

- *Belonging: Overcoming Rejection and Discovering the Freedom of Acceptance.* by Ron and Nancy Rockey, Pacific Press, 1998

- *Unbreakable Bonds* by Drs. Paul and Cheryl Meier,
- *The Rejected* by John Joseph Evoy (now out of print but occasionally available on Amazon.com)
- *Heart Connection* by Ron and Nancy Rockey, Westbow Press. Thomas Nelson, 2011. Available at www.fixablelife.com and Amazon.com.

7. Listen to audio or video seminars.

. . . and attend live seminars whenever you can.

We peel like the layers of an onion – one at a time, and sometimes we cry. The tears are appropriate too! They contain an element that, when cried from sadness, brings healing to the tissues of the body.

Whenever you have the opportunity to attend a seminar, even if you been there before and found it beneficial, attend again. Because we cannot absorb all layers of information at once (especially if it is emotionally charged) we end up missing a lot of information that might be valuable to us. We have heard from many attendees that they are returning for the second or third time because they always learn something new which causes them to peel off another layer of dysfunction.

If you have not attended a live seminar of "WHY?" or "HEART CONNECTION" this would be a great experience for you. Watch the www.fixablelife.com website for dates, times and places where seminars are being held. Also available at the above website is a LIVE seminar called "Connecting the Dots," which can be of great value to you.

8. <u>Validate your anger</u>

It's probably justified, HOWEVER, keeping it will ONLY hurt you further!

On a recent Dr. Phil show, a husband and wife in distress were his guests. The husband had left and returned again four times to his marriage. Somehow his guilt for having left his wife and three children would overtake him after he'd been gone from home for a while, so he would slink back into the marriage and to his wife's bed. She would accept him back time and again. During one of his last absences, his girlfriend had become pregnant. His own children at home knew the circumstances, were devastated to say the least, and had lost respect for their father.

The wife seemed emotionless. Dr. Phil was flabbergasted by the fact that she kept allowing him to return, and had even consented to "raise the baby as my own" who was conceived outside of her marriage, by her husband with the girlfriend. The only boundaries she had established were that she would not allow the girlfriend to continue the affair with her husband.

"Where is your rage about this? Why aren't you screaming; setting firm boundaries? Aren't you devastated, angry or hurt about this whole mess and the betrayal of yourself and your children?" Dr Phil pursued.

It was almost as if she was fearful of her own anger; afraid that she'd "go over the edge" if she once let go. She never showed the anger on stage, but was very controlled – almost blank in her affect. She had a right to rage. **You have a right to rage or cry if you have been unjustly treated or abused.** Tell yourself the truth! If you hide, repress or cover-up your negative emotions, you will not heal! And you deserve healing.

Remember the story of our nephew, Danny? Even though we pleaded with Danny to get some help, some therapy for this seething anger he felt, instructing him that anger is lethal, deadly. Unfortunately, Danny was afraid to let go, to forgive, thinking that doing so would let his father “off the hook”.

Less than a year after his mother’s funeral, Danny’s heart literally exploded in his chest. He was a thirty-two year old – a non-drinker, a non-smoker and not on drugs. That was proven at his autopsy. He literally chose his own death by choosing to hold onto his hatred.

You don’t have to be a Danny. No one does. Process through your memories, and let go of the negative emotions that do you in if you hold onto them.

Unfortunately, many people deny themselves life at its fullest by not experiencing excellent intimate relationships with their family and friends. Years go by with couples not speaking to each other, parents not speaking to children or being spoken to by them, and siblings seething instead of celebrating holidays and reunions together. WHY?

“He did me wrong,” “She never loved or cared about me anyway, so why should I care about her?” “I’ll never go to him/her! They should come to me because they owe ME an apology.” Splintered marriages and families abound and rage is on the rise!

In these messy situations, all we do is teach our children how to reject and disrespect and hate. Our acts of omission and commission get dumped onto them. It’s a NO FAIR! Of course you have the right to disagree, but not to be disagreeable! Of course you have the right to be angry; as the Bible says, "Be angry and sin not" Woops! How can you be angry without hurting others? Well, you hurt yourself instead like Danny did.

DO THIS: **Make a list of the people you are angry with, and start writing about that anger. As a matter of fact, write to the people you are angry with. Write a letter that NEVER gets sent. You see, the letter is not for revenge or retribution – it's for emptying the garbage inside of you, that shadow, that will destroy you from the inside out. You deserve to live!**

If you can, investigate the beginning experiences of the one(s) who rejected you, and you may well discover that they too were rejected. Remember, those filled with rejection, cannot pour out acceptance!

9. Mourn your losses - True sorrow is appropriate, and all the comfort of a supportive group, your church, God, family and friends is available to you!

Ena had lost her husband of thirty-eight years to a massive heart attack. While his death had been sudden, his illness had been of long standing. Jim was a severe diabetic, who walked around with an inordinately high blood sugar level almost all of the time. He took Insulin by injection because his own pancreas was not producing what he needed.

Now Jim was a highly intelligent man with a genius IQ, but when it came to his diabetes, he didn't use his intellect! He just didn't have the ability to avoid sweets and eat a diet that would have minimized his blood sugar level. Do you think that his beginnings may have contributed to his cravings? It wasn't until after his death that the family discovered just how out of control his diet was. A trip to the ice cream parlor revealed that he had been there almost every day in his life for a double-dipped, chocolate ice cream cone. Candy bars were found hidden all over his workshop and even in his pick-up truck!

Ena was devastated! For many years, every conversation was somehow turned to talking about her wonderful Jim, but she hid her anger and disappointment for years! She never spoke of the betrayal she felt by his choice to eat ice cream and all manner of sweets rather than to live a long life with her.

Finally three months prior to her death at eighty-five, she began letting her feelings out. Looking at his picture hung on the wall of her little apartment, night after night she "told him off" until finally there was no more to say. She had loved him so deeply; they had produced children together. He had been the love of her life, and she couldn't understand why eating sweets and an unhealthy diet was more important to him, than enjoying the Golden Years side by side. Once her true feelings of abandonment had surfaced and been expressed, she was at peace, and still deeply in love with him.

Ena's death came quickly and easily. There was no struggling, no regrets and nothing left unsaid. She had said it all, let out her real truth, and was ready for a peaceful departure.

Hiding truth, lying to yourself and others and sitting on negative emotions causes crippling physical and mental diseases and in some cases early death. Being honest with yourself and others and completing what feels incomplete in your life, creates harmony, joy and no regrets or struggles when life is nearly over.

DO THIS: **Remember that list you wrote a bit ago – the list of all those people who you felt rejected you? Well, now it's time to get it out.**

Choose a rainy or quiet afternoon, take the phone off the hook, and carefully examine the lost relationships there. Name by name, write what you have missed through the years because that relationship was lost. Add what it could have been if the relationship was still intact.

Then do one final thing with those names. If the persons on the list are still alive, write about your part in the demise of the relationship. Then write about what it would take to rekindle the relationship, and what you are willing to do to attempt that.

If you feel that rekindling a relationship with a specific person(s) could be dangerous, write about why you believe that. Not all relationships lost will be reconciled; in fact, some should not be because doing so would be detrimental to one or both of you.

Basically what you are doing in this step is the work that Ena did. She did it before her death. You can do it to promote your new life!

10. <u>Reframe your story</u> - understand it from a new perspective.

In the process of recovery we change our vantage point - the view is different, because **we** move!

Before recovery we look at those who wounded us or who did not bond to us <u>as a child sees.</u> A child is helpless, needy, ignorant and unable to think from cause to effect or to think in concepts. When we are wounded, we remain as children emotionally, stuck at the age that we were when the wound occurred. We develop tactics for survival – designed to get us what we think we want or need. Being demanding, controlling or manipulative are just a few survival techniques.

"You owe me, you make it all better," we say when we are emotional kids. "I am at the center of my universe, and your job as my parents is to meet all of my needs, all of my wants and everyone who knows me is to do the same." We pout when we don't get our way, or perhaps we throw a temper tantrum, demanding that we get "our due". We even threaten to leave the relationship, the meeting or the job if we don't get our own way.

As we begin the healing process and have emptied some of the pain that has been following us closely, we begin to change our perspective. We realize that no one can change us from the outside, and that the responsibility for change is placed squarely on our shoulders. Those who are religious tend to ask assistance from a "Higher Power" – Christians seek assistance from God. We come to understand that we must stop the blame game and choose recovery for ourselves. We must walk through what might be a dark or gloomy valley of memories of abandonment, of feeling unloved or unwanted, or of being raised in a chaotic environment.

At some point in the process, we begin to shift our vantage point from childhood to adulthood. Here we will switch attitudes from childish to more adult. "Oh well, you win some, you loose some. I just got the short straw this time. I can survive" we think. You see, the shadow, which contains all the negative junk left over from wounds received, begins to recede, and we can think more clearly, more adult-like. We are coming out of the darkness that the shadow has brought us.

If we choose to remain open to further self-examination and advanced understanding, we will make a final move. . .

Quite imperceptibly at first, we begin to see our parents and others who may have wounded us through the eyes of God. The Bible tells us that our behaviors are not clean, and that there is not a one who has not sinned. And it reminds us that we are all loved equally - that our acceptance is not based on performance but upon whose we are. We come to realize that our worth and value is infinite, and so is the value of those who hurt us. We begin to separate worth and value from behaviors, and that takes others off the hook too.

Little by little are hearts are softened, and we realize that those who wounded us were also wounded. They were set up by their beginnings to attach poorly, to abandon as they were abandoned or to be unable to connect emotionally. Eventually forgiveness comes and we are able to choose to pass it along to others. That lets US off the hook. Now we are free to be and to thrive!

Looking at the rejection you experienced, may require that you look in the mirror. It may require that you examine just what part you may have played in a lost relationship. That's not always so easy to do!

Granted, what you received was unfair, hurtful and has caused you much pain throughout your life; however, you may have chosen to continue a vendetta that has caused you to carry a burden far too heavy to bear. Remember Nancy's story? While still a young child, she made the choice to reject the man who was her father, a man she had not known. Yes, he was the adult and should have been able to surmount her rejection by his kindness, but his own rejection as a child, still harbored in his heart and experienced daily from his mother, prevented him from reaching out in love to his child.

DO THIS: **Look back on those who have rejected you. Acknowledge and write about the part you may have played in that standoff. Perhaps you have some things about which to forgive yourself or to ask forgiveness from those with whom you have a severed relationship.**

11. Repair the Story

DO THIS: **Understand the vicious cycles you've been on. Halt the vicious cycles.**

- **Look carefully at the survival techniques you have adopted. Are they healthy or are they destructive?**
- **Are you paying a big price in terms of lost relationships or loneliness?**
- **Are your relationships suffering?**
- **Are your children distant, not wanting to connect with you?**
- **Have you excommunicated yourself from family, friends or co-workers?**
- **What exactly are the prices you are paying?**

Answer these questions on paper. Then draw out the cycles of self-destruction that you've been on. This will help you to see the vicious cycles, and actually draw out what opposite (healthy) steps you can take instead. Once you have examined your self-destructive techniques, you will no doubt decide to make some changes, and that will be wise. Once made, you will derive benefits from

healthier techniques, and you should maximize their positive effect. Write about the changes you want to make and talk about your changes, your healing, the self-understanding that has occurred, prompting your changes. The more you capitalize on the benefits you are receiving, the more you will benefit.

Refer back to the lesson about the "Y." Take a look at the techniques that you developed in an attempt to prevent yourself from feeling the pain of rejection. Write them down and ask also what positive effects you received from these techniques or what ill effects have been yours. Write about both.

Ask yourself, then, exactly what it would take to turn from these ways that are self-destructive, and begin a new path toward victory. Write these things down, and vow to begin the process immediately. Make sure that along the way, you have the support of others who are likewise on "A Journey." Become part of a supportive group to whom you can be accountable.

12. <u>Develop boundaries</u> to prevent yourself from being re-wounded

DO THIS: **Set the boundaries firm with those who still try to abuse you. Absent yourself from them if and when the abuse starts.**

It is not wise to keep returning to the same beach where time after time, sharks attack, dismembering body limbs and causing death, all the while hoping for different results. So it is with some relationships. Those who habitually cause mayhem and destruction of your feelings, causing your behaviors to become destructive of yourself or others, are not those with whom you should consistently chum around.

In choosing companions, carefully evaluate how you react to each other. If you are frequently ignored, abandoned or emotionally abused, cease and desist! Choose others with whom you can appreciate life, and either avoid or gently confront those who cause you pain.

It took Nancy nearly a lifetime to finally stop the verbal put-downs from her mother. While her Mom was mostly a loving woman, she also was very critical of her only child in an attempt to make her perfect. Whenever in her presence, Nancy's Mother would make comments (mostly derogatory) about her appearance – *"Hair too short, to long, too gray, too blonde, too fat, too thin, gone too much, don't do enough for me etc., etc."*

About three months before her mother's death, while visiting at Mother's apartment, Mother started in again. Nancy says it this way: "I responded to her criticism like this -

Mom, that's not fair! I am your only child, and constantly you tear me apart. I can't seem to do right for doing wrong. But what you aren't thinking about is that I am doing exactly what you dreamed I would – we have a ministry. Every time we are home, I spend a lot of time with you. I take you to appointments. I buy your clothes and your food. I searched until I found the most beautiful apartment in town and here you are in it. I take you on outings and out to eat. Wherever we go to a speaking engagement, I bring something back for you and have taken you on many trips. But yet you criticize; you complain about me being gone. It's just not fair, Mom."

The criticism stopped that day. Never again did her mother say a derogatory word. Instead, she complimented and praised. On her death bed, with Nancy at her side, she repeated over and over, *"How can I bear to leave you, my precious treasure?"*

What a blessing that Nancy chose to set a boundary that day. How much better to say her final "*good-bye*" with all being at peace between them and no regrets on Nancy's part after Mother's death.

Maybe there's a few with whom you need to set a boundary. If so, do it softly, gently and kindly.

13. <u>Forgiveness is a gift received from God.</u>

We receive it as we are willing to empty ourselves of the bitterness, anger, malice, sadness etc. that have clogged the passageway between us and God – and that includes receiving forgiveness for yourself for past mistakes or misdeeds. You WILL give forgiveness to those who have wounded you, because when you receive it, it automatically flows out to others. You will receive it once you have emptied all of the negative emotion attached to the misdeed.

Remorse is the aftermath of a truly repentant heart. Every cause has an effect, and remorse is the effect of having hurt another. Even after repentance and receiving forgiveness from the one you have hurt, remorse will surface from time to time. It is simply regret that you hurt another, that you caused pain in the life. Remorse reminds us of the ravaging damage we might have created in someone's experience, and discourages us from repeating the offense.

DO THIS: **Don't try to muster up forgiveness for one who has hurt you. Instead, just be willing to receive forgiveness in your heart and mind. The**

open willing spirit will receive what it needs so that forgiveness can flow out through it to others, including oneself.

How beneficial it is here, to write about the history of the person who rejected you. If you know very little, then do some homework – ask questions and talk to others who can fill you in. When you come to know yourself and the pain you have suffered, it is amazing how clearly you come to see the pain in others. Then you can offer grace and mercy and understanding about their hurtful actions toward you. Their past does not excuse their behavior, but it certainly does provide the reason for it.

14. Consider reconciliation - This is a 2-way process that requires willingness on the other person's part. Don't force your way.

The old song says that "it takes two to tango", and the truth is that it also takes two for reconciliation to occur. It may be that the one who abandoned, neglected or rejected you does not have what it takes to make a successful relationship. Try as you will, you cannot seem to make any headway with this individual; the relationship appears doomed.

DO THIS: **It is wise to attempt to heal a broken friendship or relationship, but you cannot, on your own, make it happen. Go to the person in question and without accusing or blaming, but taking responsibility for your feelings and behaviors, seek to reconcile. If your attempts result in failing to establish interest in a relationship, realize that the other is wounded, and does not have your self-knowledge, is afraid,**

or doesn't know how to emotionally connect, just remember that you did what is proper. You may have to mourn the loss of a relationship that was important to you, but you cannot "fix" the other. You can only "fix yourself" and go on toward complete emotional health.

Reconciliation looks more like connecting or reconnecting. As you have examined yourself during these ten chapters you may have discovered that you were either avoidant and choose to not connect or ambivalent and choose to cling. Perhaps you found yourself as a combination of the two and subsequently labeled yourself as having the disorganized style of attachment because you came from an abusive background. (You can learn about Styles of Attachment in the book "Shadows of Connecting," available at www.fixablelife.com.)

You may have discovered that your attachment style is not serving you well and thus you desire to move to secure attaching. If this is true of you, study well what a secure attachment is, after you have dissected the cause of your particular style, and healed from the wounds received early in life that promoted the style you chose. Begin slowly and carefully to reconstruct your style, taking on some of the characteristics of the securely attached. Actually, you will begin that process automatically as you heal from wounds received progresses. Others will quickly notice that you no longer avoid or cling, and will wonder what has happened within you.

If you are or choose to be a Christian, DO THIS:

15. Spend time alone with God and His word - every day.

The power for the entire process comes from Him! Read uplifting Biblical passages, read inspirational material. What we take in becomes who we are. The more positive and truth-filled material we read, the more positive and truthful we will become.

Find the texts that speak of God's acceptance of His children, and allow them to comfort and encourage you.

16. Communicate with God in Prayer - AND -

Make your prayers be prayers of thanksgiving for the victory that He is giving you, even though you may not see immediate results, rather than rehearsing your sinful ways. Reliving the past over and over only imbeds your transgressions deeper into the psyche, making the habits harder to eliminate. Talk to God often, laying your concern before Him, and thanking Him for what He is accomplishing in your life. PRAISE OFTEN!

ADDED BONUS

Ron, who experienced rejection from conception on, has found these ideas to be helpful to him in his recovery process. Perhaps they will benefit you if you apply them in your recovery also.

- **Memorize and keep repeating to yourself and others this phrase** –

"WHAT WAS THEN IS NOW."

"This phrase has helped me immeasurably! Often when I feel rejection from someone or something else, rather than immediately react to it with a negative thought or behavior, I repeat, "That was then, this is now." That reminds me not to add all the rejections of the past to this little experience of the present. It also gives me a moment to ask myself if this is absolute rejection or my interpretation of the present due to the rejection filters that are still in a little shadow following me. Usually, I can relax and then my responses aren't off the wall!"

- **Identify your personal filters.**

Describe and write about them. Grey glasses? Everything black? Everyone rejecting you? Shadow still following me?

- **Identify what your rejection triggers are.**

Make a list of what sights, sounds, tastes, smells, and feelings trigger thoughts and feelings of being rejected within you. Keep the list handy. Maybe it'll be beneficial to refer to it when you are feeling rejection. Has this or that trigger set you off?

Stop when the feeling comes. Feel the feeling (frightening perhaps, but necessary). Unless we feel the feeling, we cannot identify what it is. Then ask, what triggered this feeling of ___________?

- **Study body sensations versus thoughts or intellect.**

Remember that the cells of the body hold emotional memory. When the sensation is in your body, make note of where in your body you first felt it. What memory of rejection is connected to that part of your body? Our tendency is to believe the body more than we believe the mind.

- **Walk by faith, not by feeling.**

Especially when it comes to intimate relationships, this is great advice. Here you recall the history you have with this person. Is she really rejecting me? Has she in the past, or have I just interpreted her/his behavior to be rejection?

Make a determination that this significant other will not and cannot reject you. Have faith in that special someone - that there's nothing you can do or say that will cause that person to reject you. Break into that shadow with the light of knowledge! Believe it. Tell yourself repeatedly that your history with this individual proves their love and acceptance, and, no matter what is said or done, you are going to believe their love for and acceptance of you. PERIOD! Then do something that shows you are breaking free of the haunting shadow.

Ron says it like this:

"When you are learning to drive a car, you learn that when you come to an intersection, you look to the left, then right, then left again before depressing the gas pedal. Right? Of course when you're in England, that becomes dysfunctional. Do that, and you're sure to get smacked by someone coming along at a good clip! There it's right, left, right, or else!"

The point is this: When we are hurting, when we feel rejected, we tend to fly right through the intersection without a second thought to the dangers there. We do not look at the caution signs or the red light. We just barrel straight into reaction to the injury we FEEL that we have received.

WHOA BABY! Take a breath. Do the things we've suggested before proceeding cautiously. It's the only way to go."

So, now you have tools to tighten up your nuts and bolts and to unlock the secrets that hide within the memory bank of your mind regarding rejection and its effect on you. You even have a working flashlight to give you sight – and insight! Get out the tool box frequently. Make sure the lug nuts are tight, the tires are full and so is the oil and gas tank, so that you can arrive at your destination safely, fulfilling your dream of connecting and acceptance. Be willing to identify the shadow that's following you and causing you to see dimly. Turn toward the light of hope and change, following the steps that will lead you out into the light of acceptance.

CPSIA information can be obtained
at www.ICGtesting.com
Printed in the USA
FFOW01n1043070517
35235FF

9 781456 610647